Our
Unseen
Enemy

By William L. Owens

1

Dedicated to: my son,

William L Owens, II (Chip),
and all those who seek after God
and His righteousness.

Unless otherwise noted,
the Scripture quoted in the text is the
Authorized King James Version.

Published by:

The 222 Plan Ministries
for Biblical Mentoring
Clark's Hill, SC

Printed in the
United States of America
by CreateSpace an amazon.com company.

Preface

Dr. William L. Owens has written a very comprehensive manuscript on evil spirits. Since the manuscript is scripturally based and theologically oriented, I am happy to see it published for the use of preachers and laymen.

The work is thorough and meticulous, yet practical. The book is relaxed and frank in approach to a subject that many capable writers have steered clear of. In fact, almost nothing has been written on this subject (prior to 1970), though it appears often in the Bible. W. L. Owens has given us a scholarly treatment of a much neglected subject.

A few illustrations in the text may be assailed but since they actually occurred we should review them. It always helps God's people to consider things which they have never witnessed personally. The book will be well received by most, and should be studied by all.

C. E. Autrey,

Late Professor of Evangelism
New Orleans Baptist
Theological Seminary *

---

*Publisher's Note: In June of 1970 Dr. Autrey read the manuscript and wrote the preface while conducting an evangelistic crusade in the York Baptist Association, Rock Hill, S.C.

Introduction

The rich man and all who follow their own rebellious sin nature will ultimately wind up in Hell—a place of keen consciousness and sorrow—alienated from God's love and mercy.

"Evil" is wickedness in action; it is the single greatest cause of human misery and degradation. Evil not only affects life's daily affairs, it also has a subtle and devastating effect on the physical, mental and spiritual aspects of all people. Not one part of our being is left untouched by evil's iniquitous nature.

Our task is to show that the Bible recognizes Satan as the author of evil and that he is at work in our present world through fallen angels. These angels are referred to in the Bible as evil spirits. Satan and his angels engage us in a spiritual war that is not based on flesh and blood. We reemphasize that the purpose set forth in these pages is to show what the scriptures teach about the reality and power of our unseen enemy, yesterday, today and tomorrow.

We proceed in a logical and chronological manner from Genesis to Revelation while invoking a casual writing style. But, don't let that casual style lead you to think the study is not serious. The warfare that engages us is spiritual in nature and God's church must learn to do battle in the spiritual arena. We must learn to apply the principles of God's Word in our wrestling with the princes of darkness. This book shows that God has provided a strategy for His people. We are victorious when we follow Him in obedience.

As we study, we assume the following premise: The Bible is the inspired Word of God and is in essence the sum total of His revealed truth to man. All biblical information or insight is assumed to be absolute in its revelation. One guiding principle flies like a banner over our search for truth: Scriptural verification is necessary for all reported conclusions. We take a dogmatic stand here because we are persuaded that The Bible is the believer's only sure Word from God.

Please do not look upon this study as purely academic. Instead, treat it as a personal spiritual journey de- signed to enhance your faithfulness in service to Christ. Knowledge alone doesn't make us better Christians. What we know must be earnestly applied and diligently followed.

I encourage you to pause at the end of every chapter and ask God if there is some truth you must personally apply.

TABLE OF CONTENTS

Chapter 1

SATAN AND THE
PROBLEM OF EVIL

Having assumed evil to be a universal human experience, we now focus on the primary source of our search. In the pages of The Holy Bible we see the results of evil. Choose any society recorded in scripture (including those who believe in God) and you will find sin and evil in varying degrees. Evil and wickedness appear to be synonymous results of a human race beset by the curse of sin.

The Bible reveals evil as a force that has both causes and effects. Evil ultimately causes misery to all. It affects our world both physically and spiritually. It promotes anxiety in body, soul, and spirit. But, where does it come from? Who initiated evil?

THE ORIGIN OF EVIL

The scriptures teach that evil comes as a result of willful sin. But, "What is sin?" Simply stated, sin is breaking God's perfectly revealed will. When man knowingly or ignorantly breaks God's Law, it is sin! For God says: "Whosoever committeth sin transgresseth also the law: for sin is the transgression of the law (1John 3:4)." The first act of rebellion took place before the creation of the world. Ezekiel, the prophet, recorded the historical ac- count in a book that bears his name. Consider carefully his testimony.

EZEKIEL'S TESTIMONY

Ezekiel recorded the account in chapter 28:11-19. Read carefully his divinely inspired words.

28:11 Moreover the word of the LORD came unto me, saying,

28:12 Son of man, take up a lamentation upon the king of Tyrus, and say unto him, Thus saith the Lord GOD; Thou sealest up the sum, full of wisdom, and perfect in beauty.

28:13 Thou hast been in Eden the garden of God; every precious stone [was] thy covering, the sardius, topaz, and the diamond, the beryl, the onyx, and the jasper, the sapphire, the emerald, and the carbuncle, and gold: the workmanship of thy tabrets and of thy pipes was prepared in thee in the day that thou wast created.

28:14 Thou [art] the anointed cherub that covereth; and I have set thee [so]: thou wast upon the holy mountain of God; thou hast walked up and down in the midst of the stones of fire.

28:15 Thou [wast] perfect in thy ways from the day that thou wast created, till iniquity was found in thee.

28:16 By the multitude of thy merchandise they have filled the midst of thee with violence, and thou hast sinned: therefore I will cast thee as profane out of the mountain of God: and I will destroy thee, An covering cherub, from the midst of the stones of fire.

28:17 Thine heart was lifted up because of thy beauty, thou hast corrupted thy wisdom by reason of thy brightness: I will cast thee to the ground, I will lay thee before kings, that they may behold thee.

28:18 Thou hast defiled thy sanctuaries by the multitude of thine iniquities, by the iniquity of thy traffic; therefore will I bring forth a fire from the midst of thee, it shall devour thee, and I will bring thee to ashes upon the earth in the sight of all them that behold thee.

28:19 All they that know thee among the people shall be astonished at thee: thou shalt be a terror, and never [shalt] thou [be] any more.

Many conservative Bible teachers believe that the above passage relates to more than the historical account of God's judgment upon a mere earthly king. William W. Orr, a popular expositor, says:

"As one examines the passage, it seems very evident that while the prince of Tyrus is actually addressed, the message beginning with verse 11 goes far beyond an earthly prince to the king of evil who stood behind him and prompted him in his wicked doings, even Satan himself. Notice the phrase, the anointed cherub that covereth (Ezekiel 28:14). The phrase indicates that this creature had the most esteemed position of all God's created beings. Because of sin, however, this personality, named "Lucifer," was found guilty of rebellion, and God pronounced future judgment upon him (Ezekiel 28:16)."[1]

Take note of the various phrases in verses twelve through fifteen that refer to issues beyond the capacity of a mere mortal. For example, how could the king of Tyre have been in the Garden of Eden? How could an earthly king have been set as the guardian over the mountain or throne of God? How could the earthly King of Tyre be considered "perfect in all his ways?" It appears that Orr and other expositors are right in their assessment that Ezekiel is actually referring to Lucifer who was energizing the wicked King of Tyre and using him as a pawn for evil.

ISAIAH'S TESTIMONY

For further light regarding Satan, we should consider the scriptural testimony of Isaiah 14:12-17. Contemplate these words.

> *14:12 How art thou fallen from heaven, O Lucifer, son of the morning! [How] art thou cut down to the ground, which didst weaken the nations!*
>
> *14:13 For thou hast said in thine heart, I will ascend into heaven, I will exalt my throne above the stars of God: I will sit also upon the mount of the congregation, in the sides of the north:*
>
> *14:14 I will ascend above the heights of the clouds; I will be like the most High.*
>
> *14:15 Yet thou shalt be brought down to hell, to the sides of the pit.*
>
> *14:16 They that see thee shall narrowly look upon thee, [and] consider thee, [saying], Is this the man that made the earth to tremble, that did shake kingdoms;*
>
> *14:17 [That] made the world as a wilderness, and destroyed the cities thereof; [that] opened not the house of his prisoners?*

When comparing the Isaiah passage with Ezekiel 28:16-17, it becomes apparent that both accounts are referring to Lucifer. It is even more apparent that he (Satan or Lucifer) is the source of evil. The conclusion seems unavoidable: evil has come from the very heart of Satan!

John Bunyan, a man of Puritan stock, possessed tremendous powers of spiritual perception. His writings have provided spiritual insight to thousands in every generation for hundreds of years. We should take note of how he interprets the above passages. Consider the following quote from his book "The Holy War:"

> *"Well, upon a time, there was one Diabolus, a mighty giant, made an assault upon the City of Mansoul, to take it and to make it his own habitation." This Diabolus is indeed a great and mighty prince, and yet both poor and beggarly. As to his origin, he was at first one of the servants of King Shaddai, made and taken and put by him into the most high and mighty places . . . "Well, he seeing himself thus exalted to greatness and honor, and raging his mind for higher state and degree, what doth he but begins to think with himself how he might be set up as lord over all . . . "*[2]

We may conclude that Bunyan believed Satan to be the father of evil. He further believed that God had created Lucifer a perfect being whose heart became filled with a desire for self glory at God's expense. Satan's pride-filled heart energized his willful rebellion against God's righteous authority. It must be remembered that

14

God did not make him a devil. He became the father of evil through his own willful transgression.[3]

SATAN'S KINGDOM

After Satan's rebellion, God declared him to be the king of rebellious fallen angels. God calls him the "god of this world" through the pen of Paul when writing his second epistle to the Corinthians (II Corinthians 4:4). This means that Satan is directly responsible for evil in the world. His sinister personality and power are further shown in various biblical designations. His most often used scriptural title is "Satan," and it means "adversary."[4]

Other descriptive names of Satan: "accuser of the brethren" (Revelation 12:10); "Beelzebub, the prince of the devils"(Matthew 12:24); "the deceiver of the whole world" (Revelation 12:9); "the wicked one"(Matthew 13:19); and "a liar and the father of lies" (John 8:44).

How did Satan become all that the above names imply? Did God create him that way? If not, what did he do to become the very embodiment of evil? Consider with me the original conflict for some answers.

THE CONFLICT

Life often appears to be a stage on which eternity plays out its drama. If life were such a stage, we would have two chief (but not equal) characters: God and Satan! They are seen as the epitome of opposites. On the one hand there is God, who is the great sovereign of the

15

uni- verse. He is perfect in all righteousness! Then, there is Satan, who is the very embodiment of evil.

Satan is the opposite of God in purpose. However, he is not the equal of God in either power or wisdom. Satan is only a created being whom God has been pleased to allow to have some measure of supernatural strength and worldly wisdom. Satan's strength and wisdom are residual attributes of a former glory. It was a glory of great exaltation. Lucifer may have been the chief of all angels. Now we see him shamed, branded a traitor, and cast down to earth. God allowed him to invade the innocence of Eden. He soiled it with his lies and deception. It is apparent that he is set on aborting the purposes of God, even though he lacks the ultimate power to accomplish his goal.

God draws back the veil that we may see the dawn of man's history. Here, we discover the first record of many earthly skirmishes (Genesis 3:1-19). It was in this recorded encounter that Satan shows himself to be far superior to mere human mortals. He introduced his deceptive strategy of temptation while appearing as one having holy purposes. Scripture reports that man fell as Satan applied his wiles. Having succumbed to Satan's temptation, man became subject to the king of evil.

There you have it: the first official record of the beginning of man's spiritual conflict. The conflict that began in Eden's garden will continue until God calls it all to an end.

It was in Eden that man first felt the influence of evil. When he yielded to the temptation to disobey God, he lost his standing and fellowship with God. Man became bound by the chains of sin. Therefore, God allows a great conflict to exist in the universe. It is a spiritual war between two wills in a gigantic struggle. The battlefield is the soul of man.[5] Man was lost in Eden and all born of Adam's race are still lost and under the sentence of holy judgment.

Satan is the god of this world. As the world's "god" and limited sovereign, he has power over the world system (I John 5:18-19). It is through this world system that he seeks to keep mankind bound to himself. When Satan is successful it is because of man's enslavement to sin. When Adam chose to disobey God, he sinned and that agreement with sin placed him in the rebel's camp (Roman's 5:12). However, God loved His people and provided a means by which they would be made righteous. John 3:16 declares His redemptive plan. Satan knows that if man really believes on and depends upon what the Savior did at Calvary, then he will be set free!

Our beloved Paul in writing to the church at Galatia expresses God's love for His people when he said in Galatians 1:3-4:

> *1:3 Grace [be] to you and peace from God*
> *the Father, and [from] our Lord Jesus Christ,*

1:4 Who gave himself for our sins, that he might deliver us from this present evil world, according to the will of God and our Father:

From these verses note the following details. Paul greets the church and presents the following facts: (1) God has bestowed unmerited favor upon those to whom he is writing; (2)the world in which they are living is evil; (3) through Jesus Christ, God has delivered them from the evil world.

The above facts are true for every successive generation of believers. We must rejoice over our Lord's victory!

SATAN AND THE EVIL WORLD

The greatest concern we now have is relating to "this present evil world" (Galatians 1:4). What does the scripture mean by "evil world?" Consider the thoughts of A. T. Pierson who says:

> *"Worldliness and wickedness are hardly synonymous or equivalent terms. Nine words are translated world—five in the Old Testament and four in the New. The latter four have various shades of meaning, but all may be comprised in these: two regarding the earth as a material sphere, and habitable globe; another as an exhibition of divine order. . . a cosmos—the remaining word expresses the idea of time. . . combining these meanings, the general idea suggested by the*

world is: the earth as the habitation of
man . . . but in connection with this, the notion
of that which is fleeting, passing away,
perishing."

The world is, in the Bible sense, material, visible, temporal. While man belongs to a temporal order, he also belongs to the spiritual and eternal, his better part being immaterial and invisible. We have only to put these two great classes of fact in opposition to see why this existing order is called "the present evil world."[6]

Satan and his fallen angels appear to have the upper hand. Things seem to be going his way. His system of evil is hurling through human history without significant hindrance. You may well ask, "Who are these angels who work so faithfully for Satan's success? What effect do they have upon man and his offspring?" Theologians have argued and agonized over these kinds of questions for ages.[7]

Any serious student who focuses on man-to-man relationships observes that the world has become drunk on the wine of self-centeredness. Somehow there must be a solution to man's degenerate state. Before we consider God's solution, let us continue our pursuit of understanding how evil invades human life.

STUDY QUESTIONS

Chapter 1

1. What is the source of evil?

2. Without considering the Devil, who committed the first sin?

3. What part did Satan have in the process?

4. Why is Satan called the "god of this world?"

5. To what degree is Satan a sovereign? (Is his sovereignty limited? If so, why?)

NOTES

Chapter I

1 William W. Orr, The Mystery of Satan (Wheaton: Scripture Press, 1966), p.3

2 John Bunyan, The Holy War (London: Frederick Warne and Company, N.D.), p. 3

3 Herbert W. Lockyer, All the Doctrines of the Bible (Grand Rapids: Zondervan Publishing House, 1964, pp. 133-134

4 W. E. Vine, Dictionary of New Testament Words (New Jersey: F. H. Revell Co., 1966), p. 321

5 Ruth Paxson, Life on the Highest Plane (Chicago: Moody Press, 1928), Vol. 1, p. 104

6 Arthur T. Pierson, The Bible and Spiritual Life (Fincastle, Va.: Scripture Truth Book Co., 1968), p. 135-140

7 Augustus H. Strong, Systematic Theology (Philadelphia: Judson Press, 1945), p. 447

Chapter II

EVIL SPIRITS IN
THE OLD TESTAMENT

As we think about Satan and evil, we must not overlook demon spirits. We alluded to them in the previous chapter, but now we want to consider the testimony of the scriptures as to their reality. The scriptures identify them as allies of Satan and active in human history. As we search the pages of The Holy Bible, we discover many incidences where evil spirits are involved with mankind. Let us consider several of these accounts for the purpose of showing that the Old Testament scriptures recognize the reality of supernatural beings at work in man's history.

How do the agents of evil affect mankind? To give a biblical answer to that question, I identify the agents of evil as Satan and those fallen angels known as evil spirits. God will not answer all of our questions, for it is not His purpose to satisfy our curious whims for spiritual knowledge. However, He is interested in our having the information necessary to effectively and personally engage ourselves in spiritual warfare.

Focus your attention on the scriptures. Let us examine the biblical accounts of evil spirits and their influence on man. Some readers are probably trying to decide whether or not they can really bring themselves to believe that evil spirits are real. We have been so conditioned by our rationalistic society that we tend to reject anything that smacks of the supernatural.

Consider the words of a veteran missionary, John L. Nevis, a recognized authority in the field of demonism. He comes out of the Presbyterian denomination which is not given to spectacular or extravagant interpretations. He is rather reserved in describing his personal experiences. In writing about demons, he said: "Early books of the Old Testament make frequent reference to persons who had familiar spirits."[1] He further said, "Christian writers who reject the doctrine of demon possession are led to put strained interpretations on these passages."[2] In light of Nevis' statements, we proceed on the assumption that the Bible is to be interpreted as we would any other document. We will take it at face value. Most people would understand the method to be a literal approach where God is concerned with communicating His truth in a straight-forward manner.

MOSES ENCOUNTERS DEMONS

The first major historical reference to evil spirits, other than the person of Satan, is found in Exodus 7:10-11. Read the account carefully:

> *7:10 And Moses and Aaron went in unto Pharaoh, and they did so as the LORD had commanded: and Aaron cast down his rod before Pharaoh, and before his servants, and it became a serpent.*

> *7:11 Then Pharaoh also called the wise men and the sorcerers: now the magicians of Egypt, they also did in like manner with their enchantments.*

The passage relates the event which followed God's call to Moses. Almighty God called Moses to become Israel's first national spokesman and leader. The people were in grievous bondage to the Egyptians (Exodus 3:1-4,17). This first command to Moses was a difficult assignment. He was told to declare God's ultimatum to Egypt's mighty Pharaoh.

The message instructed Pharaoh to allow God's children to go into the wilderness apart from Egypt that they might offer a sacrifice of worship to Israel's God Jehovah (Exodus 5:1). The request was continually rejected and a spiritual battle followed. It was in this conflict that we dis- cern the supernatural activity of evil beings. God instructed Moses to have Aaron cast his rod upon the ground. The rod was suddenly transformed into a serpent. Pharaoh summoned his magicians. They mimicked the miracle by casting their rods upon the ground. Upon striking the ground, their rods also became serpents (Exodus 7:1-11).

The magicians and sorcerers were religious men who had been specifically trained for their work. They were probably Egyptian priests who were the only ones who understood the art of writing and interpreting their sacred hieroglyphics.[3] Most scholars believe that they were experienced in the magical art of legerdemain and related occult sorceries. This is implied by the Hebrew "lehatim" which is translated in the Authorized Version as "enchantments."[4] The supernatural element which may support the work of evil spirits in this occurrence evolves around the rods of the magicians being turned into serpents. On this issue scholars are divided. Some students of the Bible take the position that the transformation was merely the result of an Egyptian trick which could be explained naturally. One commentary states:

"The magicians of Egypt in modern times have been long-celebrated adepts in charming serpents, and particularly by pressing the nape of the neck, they throw them into a kind of catalepsy, which renders them stiff and immovable - thus seeming to change them into a rod. "...and so it appears that they succeeded by their 'enchantment' in practicing an illusion on the senses."[5]

However, I feel the above explanation does not do justice to the text because the natural reading implies the acts of the magicians were of a similar nature as that of Aaron. It does not accept the account at face value. In his work on demons, Merrill F. Unger refers to this same passage and contends that, while magic was used, it does not mean that there was an absence of supernatural power. He calls this feat a miracle of evil supernaturalism.[6] Nevis concurs with Unger when he says, "It is noticed that we have here a record, not of beliefs or superstitions, either of Jews or Egyptians, but visible facts, inseparably linked with one of the most important events in Jewish history."[7]

A. W. Pink refutes the position that the magicians were resorting to mere magical arts when he says, "Have such men forgotten those words in Revelation 16:14 — they are the spirits of demons working miracles!"[8] He further summarizes the incident as it is related to history in the following statement:

> "...The Lord permitted Pharaoh's sorcerers to work these miracles. They serve to illustrate the activities of Satan ... describing the character of his works ... exposing both the methods he pursues and the limits of his success. The Lord's servants had performed miracles - the Devil is ever an imitator - very well, the king would summon his magicians and show that they could do likewise. This exemplifies an unchanging principle in the workings of Satan. First, he seeks to oppose

with force (persecution, etc.) as he had the Hebrews by means of their slavery. When he is foiled here, he resorts to subtler methods and employs his wiles to deceive."[9]

I concur with Unger, Nevius and Pink, the passage, when taken at face value, supports the view that spiritual forces were at war in a physical and historical setting. As we continue our Old Testament search, we will discover an even more direct reference to Satan and evil spirits.

DEVIL WORSHIP

In Leviticus 17:7 Israel is warned not to worship the Devil. God gives a direct command regarding the offering of sacrifices: "And they shall no more offer their sacrifices unto devils, after whom they have played the harlot. This shall be a statute forever unto them throughout their generations (Leviticus 17:7)."

This verse is part of the body of instruction God had given to the children of Israel regarding principles of worship. Jehovah's instructions are not to be taken lightly. However, that is exactly what Israel had done. These particular instructions were needed because the people had come out of Egypt where they had been religiously corrupted.[10] Exhortations such as these contained direct commands from God. He dealt with specifics and His people were not to offer sacrifices to devils! No exceptions! God is a jealous God and will not tolerate His people worshiping at the feet of Satan through demon worship.

30

Who or what were these devils? Were they evil spirits? We must face these questions, if we are to successfully continue our investigation. In reference to Leviticus 17:7 Geerhardus Vos states: ". . . demon worship might be interpreted as of Egyptian origin." The offering of sacrifices to demons was idolatrous; hence God commanded that sacrifices be slain before the door of the tabernacle. The purpose of slaying their sacrifices at the entrance of the tabernacle was to prevent some of the Israelites from going into the wilderness and offering sacrifices unto devils. The Hebrew word rendered "devils" in this verse means "he-goats" or "hairy-ones." These were idols or forms of goat-like statues which the Egyptians and other ancient nations worshiped as gods.[11] Merrill Unger writes about the same passage:

"Etymologically the word means "hairy-one or 'he-goat' which is evidence that the Israelites considered the demonic conceptions to be goat-like in aspect or attributes. In poetic passages, Isaiah, portrays these demon-satyrs as dancing in the ruins of Babylon, and calling to one another in the desolated city (Isaiah 13:21; 34:14). The translation of 'seirim' in both of these passages by 'daimonia' is conclusive that Alexandrian Jews considered them to be demons."[12]

We see the same warning in the New Testament passage: I Corinthians 10:20, where Paul warns Corinthian believers against offering sacrifices to demons. It seems clear that there is in this historical situation an element of evil influence in idol worship. Every practice of idolatry, regardless of the culture, comes as the direct influence of "evil spirits."

THE WITCH OF ENDOR

In I Samuel 28:7-14 God provides us a passage which yields further information about evil spirits in biblical history:

> *28:7 Then said Saul unto his servants, Seek me a woman that hath a familiar spirit, that I may go to her, and inquire of her. And his servants said to him, Behold, [there is] a woman that hath a familiar spirit at Endor.*
>
> *28:8 And Saul disguised himself, and put on other raiment, and he went, and two men with him, and they came to the woman by night: and he said, I pray thee, divine unto me by the familiar spirit, and bring me [him] up, whom I shall name unto thee.*
>
> *28:9 And the woman said unto him, Behold, thou knowest what Saul hath done, how he hath cut off those that have familiar spirits, and the wizards, out of the land: wherefore then layest thou a snare for my life, to cause me to die?*

28:10 And Saul sware to her by the LORD, saying, [As] the LORD liveth, there shall no punishment happen to thee for this thing.

28:11 Then said the woman, Whom shall I bring up unto thee? And he said, Bring me up Samuel.

28:12 And when the woman saw Samuel, she cried with a loud voice: and the woman spake to Saul, saying, Why hast thou deceived me? for thou [art] Saul.

28:13 And the king said unto her, Be not afraid: for what sawest thou? And the woman said unto Saul, I saw gods ascending out of the earth.

28:14 And he said unto her, What form [is] he of? And she said, An old man cometh up; and he [is] covered with a mantle. And Saul perceived that it [was] Samuel, and he stooped with [his] face to the ground, and bowed himself.

This passage is one of the most important we will consider. Why? Because it establishes the fact that "familiar spirits" were real to the children of Israel. Here we see a backsliding Israel in a state of open rebellion. Saul has disregarded the Lord's command not to consort or traffic with familiar spirits. We must remember this biblical principle: "As the leader goes, so goes the nation."

These verses depict King Saul in a state of extreme anxiety. The Prophet Samuel, his spiritual counselor, was dead. God would not answer his call for help because of unconfessed sin. Therefore, he was without counsel from any normal source. At any moment, the Philistines were ready to attack. In his desperation he leaned unto his own understanding.[13]

Saul's situation was acute and he acted in desperation. He made the decision to consult a woman who had a 'familiar spirit.' He made this decision with full knowledge that it was contrary to God's will. This is indicated by the action he took in verse three. He followed God's orders by cutting off all wizards and those who possessed "familiar spirits" (Exodus 22:18; Leviticus 20:27). His sinfulness was amplified when he turned to the witch of Endor whom he discovered had escaped his purge. Thus, he violated Jehovah's holy command. Our interpretation of the passage turns on verse seven. If evil spirits are active in the event, studying it will assist us in our understanding. We must determine whether the woman alluded to is truly a medium or one who merely "claimed" to have the power to call back the spirits of the dead.

William Kelly believes this woman to be a medium who allowed herself to be used as an instrument of a demon. But, he qualifies the power of a medium by stating, "She only looked for the spirit that she was used to

—the demon in the New Testament language which impersonated whosoever was named."[14] Kelly believes that God took the situation out of Satan's control by allowing Samuel to present himself and to pronounce Saul's doom. He says, "It is not in the power of the devil to bring up the spirits either of the lost or the blest."[15] The Hebrew word "ob" means a skin-bottle and came to be applied to a man or woman possessed by a spirit of necromancy. Apparently the medium, when possessed with the demon, became like a bottle or sheath to this spirit.[16]

Even though she was not allowed to indulge in her satanic act, it is almost conclusive that a person possessed of an evil spirit was involved in this historical incident. The Bible warns of the danger of conversing with evil spirits (Deut. 18:10-12). One reason Saul lost his life was because he did not heed this admonition given by God (I Chronicles 10:13-14).

DEMON WORSHIP AND MANASSEH

The next passage of interest is II Kings 21:6, a verse relating to the religious practice of King Manasseh (II Kings 21:6): "And he made his son pass through the fire, and observed times, and used enchantments, and dealt with familiar spirits and wizards: he wrought much wickedness in the sight of the LORD, to provoke [him] to anger."

Some have thought that Manasseh was the most wicked of all the kings of Judah. While this may be debated, it is certainly true that he was a wicked man. Manasseh spent fifty-two years tearing down all the acts of righteousness and good that his father Hezekiah (a good king) had established.

It is not surprising to find this man trafficking with evil spirits in their various manifestations. The New Bible Commentary records that Manasseh on one occasion sacrificed his son and from Babylonian religion introduced all the evil of divination and medium-ship.[17] This wicked king went so far in his evil that he "observed clouds" and "observed serpents." This has reference to some manner of magical art which was prompted by evil spirits. He used the muttered spell or charms, and he appointed a necromancer and wizard to high office.[18] Unger says: "A considerable portion of Manasseh's guilt, in his abominable idolatrous orgy, is traceable to his trafficking with familiar spirits and wizards. He had communication with divining demons and wizard (asah ob we yid onim), that is, trafficked in divining mediums and wizards."[19]

SUMMARY

These four events in the history of God's people show that in the Old Testament there was an active influence of evil spirits.[20] The supernatural powers of these spirits were real to Moses, to the Levitical priests, to Saul, and to Manasseh. In each case God gave a warning, and when the warning was not heeded, judgment followed. The more God's people deviated from worshiping Him as they were commanded, the more susceptible they became to demonic power. In this age of grace, we too must realize that God will not tolerate His people trafficking with evil spirits. Sure chastisement will follow, if we disobey. Therefore, get rid of any devices related to superstitions and the like, for these items may be used by the enemy to destroy your testimony for Christ.

STUDY QUESTIONS
Chapter 2

1. How did Moses encounter demon activity?

2. Where in the Bible does God forbid His people from engaging in demonic activity?

3. Who sought the counsel of the "witch" of Endor and why?

4. Who was Manasseh and how was he involved in demon worship?

NOTES
Chapter 2

1 John L. Nevis, Demon Possession (Grand Rapids: Kregel Publications, 1968), p. 291

2 Ibid., p. 291

3 W. M. Thomson, The Land and the Book (Grand Rapids: Baker Book House, 1966), p. 149

4 Charles J Ellicott (ed.), Commentary on the Whole Bible (Grand Rapids: Zondervan Publishing House, 1959), Vol. I, p. 212

5 R. Jamieson, A. R. Fausset and D. Brown, Commentary on the Whole Bible (London: Oliphants Ltd, 1961), p. 59

6 Merrill F. Unger, Biblical Demonology (Wheaton Ill., Scripture Press, 1967),pp. 111-112. 7 Nevis, op. cit., p. 291

8 A. W. Pink, Gleanings in Exodus (Chicago: Moody Press), p. 61

9 Ibid., p. 62

10 Gerhards Vos, Biblical Theology (Grand Rapids: Eerdman Publishing Co., 1948), p. 127

11 Ellicott, op. cit., Vol. I, p. 212

12 Unger, op. cit., p. 60

13 G. F. Maclear, Old Testament History (Grand Rapids: Eerdman Publishing Co., 1952), pp. 313-314

14 W. Kelly, The Earlier Historical Books (Orange, California: Ralph E. Welch Foundation, N. D.), pp. 335-336

15 Ibid., p. 336

16 F. Davidson, A.M. Stibbs, and E. F. Kevan, New Bible Commentary (Grand Rapids: Eerdman Publishing Co., 1955), p. 278

17 Ibid., p. 330

18 Ellicott, op. cit., Vol. III, p. 439 19 Unger, op. cit. p. 147

20 For a list of Old Testament reference which may be helpful for independent study, refer to the appendix.

Chapter III

EVIL SPIRITS IN THE
NEW TESTAMENT

Our purpose is to establish the fact that biblical characters in the New Testament recognized the reality of evil spirits. In Old Testament history evil spirits were real to those who were affected, but few details were available concerning their characteristics. In the New Testament even the most casual reader may see that the opposite is true. Many details can be gleaned from the record of historical events. Let us look at several which depict evil spirits at work among those who lived during the time of the New Testament.

DEMONS AND CONFESSORS OF FAITH

Matthew records a portion of scripture popularly known as the "Sermon on the Mount" (Matthew 5:1-7;27). The sermon deals with many areas of life related to the "Kingdom of God." In Matthew 7:21-23 Christ prophetically mentions evil spirits:

> *7:21 Not every one that saith unto me, Lord, Lord, shall enter into the kingdom of heaven; but he that doeth the will of my Father which is in heaven.*

> *7:22 Many will say to me in that day, Lord, Lord, have we not prophesied in thy name? and in thy name have cast out devils? and in thy name done many wonderful works?*

> *7:23 And then will I profess unto them, I never knew you: depart from me, ye that work iniquity.*

Clearly, Christ rebuked those who merely professed to be Christians. He says He will condemn such professors even though they claim to have cast out devils in His name. Note the word "devils." The editors of the New Scofield Reference Bible refer to this word in the following remark: "Although the Greek 'daimonia' is generally translated 'devils' in the King James Version, 'demons' is correct."[1]

The respected English expositor, W. E. Vines, further comments on the word translated "devils." He says, "In

44

the New Testament it denotes an evil spirit."[2] Those with whom Christ dealt knew the reality of supernatural beings and some claimed to have the power to cast them out.[3]

THE POSSESSED MAN

We also observe the influence of evil spirits in Mark 5:1-13 where Jesus deals with a demon possessed man who was considered mentally deranged by the towns people:

> *5:1 And they came over unto the other side of the sea, into the country of the Gadarenes.*
>
> *5:2 And when he was come out of the ship, immediately there met him out of the tombs a man with an unclean spirit,*
>
> *5:3 Who had [his] dwelling among the tombs; and no man could bind him, no, not with chains:*
>
> *5:4 Because that he had been often bound with fetters and chains, and the chains had been plucked asunder by him, and the fetters broken in pieces: neither could any [man] tame him.*
>
> *5:5 And always, night and day, he was in the mountains, and in the tombs, crying, and cutting himself with stones. 5:6 But when he*

saw Jesus afar off, he ran and worshipped him,

5:7 And cried with a loud voice, and said, What have I to do with thee, Jesus, [thou] Son of the most high God? I adjure thee by God, that thou torment me not.

5:8 For he said unto him, Come out of the man, [thou] unclean spirit.

5:9 And he asked him, What [is] thy name? And he answered, saying, My name [is] Legion: for we are many. 5:10 And he besought him much that he would not send them away out of the country.

5:11 Now there was there nigh unto the mountains a great herd of swine feeding.

5:12 And all the devils besought him, saying, Send us into the swine, that we may enter into them.

5:13 And forthwith Jesus gave them leave. And the unclean spirits went out, and entered into the swine: and the herd ran violently down a steep place into the sea, (they were about two thousand;) and were choked in the sea.

Notice, particularly, verses two and twelve. These verses refer to the same personality, yet different terminology is used. The word "devils," refers to evil spirits. The term "unclean spirits" is probably a designation of the type of evil spirit.

The historical setting for this event opens with Christ and His disciples crossing the Sea of Galilee in their ship. Arriving on shore, they entered the forbidden land of Gadara. It was a district on the eastern shore of the Sea of Galilee.[4] It was infamous at that time because of the one possessed of evil spirits. He was referred to as the demoniac. H. A. Ironside, the popular Bible teacher of past years, says, "The demoniac was violent in character, a wild, untamable man, made such by the evil powers that possessed him."[5] The highly respected English pastor, G. Campbell Morgan, acknowledges that evil spirits possessed the man spoken of in this passage and shows that Christ acknowledged the reality of evil spirits by conversing with them and casting them out.[6]

THE POSSESSED DAMSEL

In Acts 16:16-18 the Apostle Paul deals with a young woman possessed by an evil spirit:

> *16:16 And it came to pass, as we went to prayer, a certain damsel possessed with a spirit of divination met us, which brought her masters much gain by soothsaying:*
>
> *16:17 The same followed Paul and us, and cried, saying, These men are the servants of*

47

the most high God, which show unto us the
way of salvation.

16:18 And this did she many days. But Paul,
being grieved, turned and said to the spirit, I
command thee in the name of Jesus Christ to
come out of her. And he came out the same
hour.

Briefly, the historical setting of these verses may be summarized as follows: Paul and others who were propagating the gospel settled in Philippi. Apparently, no synagogue was located in this village, but they found a place where people came together for prayer, presumably at predetermined times. On the way to one of these prayer sessions a young slave girl followed them and persisted in shouting out to the people in the streets. She told the people that Paul and the other disciples were servants of the most high God. The girl followed this procedure for many days. It continued until Paul, in the name of Christ, cast out the evil spirit that was possessing her.[7]

In the quoted text , two phrases are of utmost importance. Note the phrase, "a certain damsel possessed with a spirit of divination" (Acts 16:16). In order to justifiably place this event with those which involve evil spirits, we must determine the meaning of this portion of the verse. The remarks of David Thomas, a famous conservative Bible scholar of another era, will help the research at this point:

"A certain damsel possessed with a spirit of divination, or as the margin reads, of Python. In the Greek mythology that was the name of a serpent which guarded an oracle on Mount Parnassus, and was slain by Apollo, thence called Pythius, as being himself the god of divination. That she was not as some suppose, a mere ventriloquist, or lunatic, but a demoniac, is clear from Paul's response to her."[8]

It is clear that Thomas sees this damsel as one who is under the control of an evil spirit. Further enlightenment is offered by Elicott when he says,

"The fact that Luke. . . should here use this exceptional description seems to imply either that this was the way in which the people in Philippi spoke of the maiden, or else that he recognized in her phenomena identical with those of the priestesses of Delphi . . . the madness of an evil inspiration."[9]

The other phrase upon which the study focuses is "Paul . . . said to the spirit . . ." (Act 16:18) . Thomas says of these words, "Her deliverance from the evil spirit was miraculous and instantaneous."[10] The Greek word, "pneuma," which has been translated "spirit," refers to an immaterial personality which has the power of knowing, deciding, desiring, and acting. This particular "spirit" is a spirit higher than man but lower than God.[11] Therefore, we conclude with confidence that this slave

49

girl was possessed with an evil spirit. Two logical reasons for acceptng this position are: (1) Luke, in recording the event, recognizes the girl is possessed to the extent that he identifies the demon; (2) Paul, in casting out the evil spirit, addresses the spirit personally. Both Paul and Luke in describing their experience, related to evil spirits as personal beings.

Next Sunday

JEWISH EXORCISTS

When considering demons we should also investigate the historical event recorded in Acts 19:13-16:

> *13 Then certain of the vagabond Jews, exorcists, took upon them to call over them which had evil spirits the name of the Lord Jesus, saying, We adjure you by Jesus whom Paul preacheth.*
>
> *19:14 And there were seven sons of [one] Sceva, a Jew, [and] chief of the priests, which did so.*
>
> *19:15 And the evil spirit answered and said, Jesus I know, and Paul I know; but who are ye? 19:16 And the man in whom the evil spirit was leaped on them, and overcame them, and prevailed against them, so that they fled out of that house naked and wounded.*

Paul, as an apostle, was clearly a man of God. He honored his call from God to be an apostle to the gentiles. God confirmed Paul's appointment by granting him apostolic authority. This authority included performing miracles to confirm his God-given message. Why did God do this? Because, at that moment in history the Bible had not been completed. Those books of scripture that were available were only accessible to the religious scholars and perhaps to some among the privileged and well educated.

God temporarily confirmed His message of propositional truth through miracles. Until the Bible was completed, the only propositional truth available to the man in the street was the prophet of God. When the prophet spoke God allowed some miracles to be performed to affirm that the prophet was speaking for God. These verses in Acts 19 clearly depict Paul's unusual anointing. He was in the city of Ephesus ministering to the diverse needs of the people when God wrought special miracles by his hands. Because of this, special anointing, people were healed and evil spirits departed from them. Then some Jews thought to be of lower class, appeared on the scene and sought to cast out an evil spirit. However, the spirits challenged and attacked them. At this demonstration of demonic boldness the vagabond Jews fled.

Let's look at two particular verses which directly mention evil spirits. The first speaks of the vagabond Jews and their desire to cast out the evil spirits (Acts 19:13). Nevis says, "Exorcists are specially hated by the evil spirits."[12] Those vagabond Jews were men who undertook to dispel demons by the use of spells or charms; some of these spells or charms, according to Josephus, are said to have been handed down from Solomon.

When Christ was conducting His earthly ministry, these itinerant exorcists were numerous.[13] For some, exorcism was a regular occupation. There is no reason to doubt that these recorded events actually took place.[14] Why did these wonder working sons of Sceva use the name of Christ as they attempted to cast out the demon? They probably had heard Paul invoke the name of Christ and desired to try its authority for themselves.[15] They sought to use the name of Christ just as they had used other charms and enchantments to their success. These sons of Sceva saw the name of Jesus as just another magical formula by which to line their pockets with financial gain.

The second illustrates the fact that evil spirits actually spoke (Acts 19:15). Note the phrase, "Jesus I know, and Paul I know. . ." Concerning this phrase, Ellicott says:

> *"Better, 'Jesus I acknowledge'. The two verbs are different in the Greek, the one implying recognition of authority, the latter, as colloquially used, though originally it had a stronger meaning, a more familiar acquaintance. The possessed man, identifying himself, as the Gadarene did, with the demon, stood in awe of the Name of Jesus, when uttered by a man like St. Paul: but who were*

*these seven pretenders that they should usurp
authority over him?"[16]*

Ellicott was convinced that an evil spirit was actually
speaking. The study of Acts 19:13-16 supplies us with
conclusive evidence that on this particular missionary
journey Paul encountered demonic activity in an unusual
way.

SUMMARY

We have now seen enough cases to establish the fact
that evil spirits were real to those who lived in the New
Testament era. Many other cases could be cited but little
could be added to offer strength to our premise.[17] Two of
the historical cases were incidents in the life of Christ, in
which He acknowledged and dealt with evil spirits. The
other events were found to be part of the historical
account of Paul's missionary journeys.

We learned that the personalities involved in these
events dealt with evil spirits as a real phenomenon.
According to the most reliable sources of history, evil
spirits in the New Testament era manifested themselves
in several ways.[18] Demons were not merely superstitious
or imaginative figures of those who encountered them.

STUDY QUESTIONS

Chapter 3

1. What did Jesus have to say about mere professors of faith?

2. Do you believe the man in Mark 5:1-13 was demon possessed or insane? Why?

3. Why did Paul rebuke the demon possessed girl?

4. How does the case in Acts 19:13-16 show demonic activity?

END NOTES

Chapter 3

1 C. I. Scofield, New Scofield Reference Bible, (ed.) E. S. English, (New York: Oxford Press, 1967) p. 1003

2 W. E. Vine, Expository Dictionary of New Testament Words (Westwood, N.J.: F. H. Revell Co., 1940) p. 291

3 R. Jamieson, A. R. Fausett, and D. Brown, Commentary on the Whole Bible (London: Oliphants Ltd., 1961), p. 912

4 F. Davidson, A. M. Stibbs, and E. F. Kevan, The New Bible Commentary (Grand Rapids: Eerdman Publishing Co., 1955), p. 784

5 Harry A. Ironside, Expository Notes on Mark (Nepture, N. J.: Loizeaux Brothers, Inc., 1948) p. 77

6 G. Campbell Morgan, The Gospel According to Mark (Westwood, N. J. : F. H. Revell Co., 1927) pp. 110-117

7 F. Davidson, et. al. op. cit., p. 291

8 David Thomas, Acts of the Apostles (Grand Rapids: Baker Book House, 1955), p. 253

9 Charles J. Ellicott (ed.), Commentary on the Whole Bible (Grand Rapids: Zondervan Publishing House, 1959) Vol. VII, p. 106

10 Thomas, op. cit., p. 253

11 Joseph H. Thayer, Greek-English Lexicon of the New Testament (Grand Rapids: Zondervan Publishing House, 1962) p. 250

12 John L. Nevis, Demon Possession (Grand Rapids: Kregel Publications, 1968)p. 70

13 Thomas, op cit., p. 313

14 Williams Barclay, The Acts of the Apostles (Philadelphia: Westminister Press, 1955) p. 156

15 Thomas, op. cit., p. 313

16 Ellicott, op cit., p. 130

17 A list of New Testament references dealing with evil spirits may be found in the appendix

18 Alfred Edersheim, Jesus the Messiah (New York: Longmans, Green, and Co., 1898) pp. 479-480

Chapter IV

THE CHARACTER
OF EVIL SPIRITS

In Chapter One we discovered that evil spirits are under the supervision of Satan. We also found that Satan is the author of all evil. We further discovered that he is a king or ruler of an empire, and that he is man's greatest spiritual threat. Granting that these facts are true, we can conclude that the traits of Satan's personality and those of evil spirits are essentially the same. E. M. Bounds in his book on Satan says, "He (Satan) is a great manager. He manages bad men, often good men and bad angels."[1] In a summary statement, Bounds reveals his remarkable perception and ability to recognize the primary character of evil spirits:

The devil and his angels are of a higher order than the fallen sons of Adam, by rank, order, and intelligence. The devil is called in the Bible a prince, a world ruler, 'prince of this world.' He is designated as 'the devil and his angels.' He and they are held accountable, are condemned for their sins and for revolt in leaving their 'first estate,' the sphere for which they were created, and in which they were originally placed by God. This fact of their fall, and all other statements, direct and incidental, emphasize them as persons, living, acting, free, accountable. That they had a chief prince in all their movements, prince in wisdom, prince in skill, and in leadership, is clear from all scriptural statements concerning the devil and his angels.[2]

ORIGIN OF EVIL SPIRITS

The scriptures do not give us a direct statement about the origin of evil spirits, except that they are created beings. They are angels that sinned. This fact is known because they are identified with Satan, the father of sin (Matthew 24:41). Here is scriptural proof that Satan and evil spirits are personalities. The Bible is perfectly clear about this fact. On one occasion the Jews accused Jesus of casting out demons by the power and authority of Beelzebub who is the prince demons. The Lord Jesus, in reply to this accusation, said, "Every kingdom divided against itself is brought to desolation . . . and if Satan cast out Satan, he is divided against himself; how shall then his kingdom stand?" (Matthew 12:25-26). Christ recognized evil spirits as real personalities.

What about the makeup of these beings, their number, their intelligence, their power? The answers to such queries can be gleaned only in scripture. God has not revealed to us all we may wish to know of these spirits. He has withheld certain information for purposes known only to Himself. The spirit realm is a mystery which will be revealed unto man when God wills to do so. For the time being, we must be content with God's present revelation on this subject.

DEMONS ARE SPIRITS

A thorough scrutiny of the Bible discloses that evil spirits are spiritual in nature (Luke 10: 17-20). Demons are immaterial; that is, they cannot be physically touched or felt. Merrill F. Unger in his excellent work on demonology states, "Demons, hence, are scripturally presented as purely spiritual beings."[3] He further says, "The specific attribute of 'spirit' is then immateriality, incorporeality. . . but it must not be supposed that because spirits are immaterial, they are any less personal."[4] In a pure sense, demons or evil spirits are spiritual beings that operate above the natural laws of the physical universe. They are not subject to restrictions placed upon humans and are, therefore, supernatural.

While demons are spirit beings, there are indications in scripture that they may have the ability to take material form. For instance, God is a spirit, and He incarnated Himself as the God-man, taking a body which had form (John 1:14). There are also incidents in scripture where angels took physical form in their service for God. Angels in human form warned Lot of the destruction of Sodom (Genesis 19:1). On another occasion an angel of God released Peter from Jail as other believers prayed for his release or deliverance (Acts 12:9). While all or some of these may have been Theophanies, the fact remains the supernatural on occasions may appear as natural.

When God permits it, there is no reason to believe that demons cannot take physical form and thereby become visible to man. However, the key rests in God's sovereignty! His will must be obeyed or the consequences must be paid. Even evil spirits must yield when and where God has declared man off limits to their Satanic tactics.

DEMONS ARE INTELLIGENT BEINGS

Evil spirits are intelligent beings; they are knowledgeable and wise (1Kings 22:22-24; Acts 16:16). They are superhuman in their knowledge to the point that they can foretell the future. Their foreknowledge is, of course, limited by the will of God.[5] It is clear that evil spirits have knowledge and intellectual understanding, yet they do not have saving knowledge (James 2:19).

Augustus H. Strong, the eminent Baptist theologian, says: "Evil spirits are confirmed in evil."[6] They will never change their minds for their hearts are set. Dr. Strong further says, "They (Evil spirits) are personal — that is — intelligent and voluntary agents."[7] Evil spirits realize that Christ is the Savior of mankind (Mark 5:7), and they are aware of the fact that He is the eternal Master of the universe. In this sense they know Christ; however, they are merely acknowledging a higher authority, and their attitude toward Jesus is one of resentment and hate.[8]

SATANIC ORGANIZATION

The scripture indicates that evil spirits are numerous. For example, a man in the district of Gadara was possessed by a "legion" of evil spirits (Mark 5:1-18). These spirits, which are great in number, are organized into a Satanic government.

Satan has fashioned his kingdom into "principalities . . .powers, . . .sovereigns of this present darkness" (Ephesians 6:12). A review of topical verses reveals an evil hierarchy. The verse reads "Satan's throne . . .where Satan dwelleth" (Revelation 2:13). His method of ranking is mentioned as his "ministers" (II Corinthians 11:15), his "principalities," his "powers," and his "hosts of evil spirits" in the heavens (Ephesians 6:12).

These descriptions seem to indicate that Satan has demons delegated to specific positions and areas of authority. We may also infer that demons are not equal in ability. We conclude that Satan's kingdom is vast and intricate in its organization.

THE IMMORAL NATURE OF DEMONS

Focusing on the immoral nature of demons, one asks: "How can their morality be determined?" We discover the nature of the personalities of evil spirits by studying the names and titles given to Satan.

The traits of demons are similar to those of their king. In the scriptures, the most often used term for Satan is his name, which means "adversary." Therefore, one of the characteristics of evil spirits is that they are rebellious. They fight against the purpose of God (Matthew 13:36-43). The Greek noun "antidikos," translated "adversary" in most New Testament passages, means "an opponent in a lawsuit." This word also denotes an adversary or an enemy without regard to legal matters. This latter definition is perhaps its meaning in 1 Peter 5:8 where it is used of Satan.[9] Evil spirits, as Satan's messengers, are the adversaries of God. Demons are war-like opponents of good and righteousness.

In Matthew 4:3 the devil is referred to as the "tempter." The title connotes malicious wickedness. Other titles indicating the same moral nature are: "the wicked one" (Matthew 13:38) and "fowler" (Psalm

91:3). These names indicate extreme wickedness. Webster's New Collegiate Dictionary defines wickedness as "morally bad or evil" and "likely to cause harm or trouble."

Other distinguishing terms used in describing Satan may be grouped together. These terms are: "wolf" (John 10:12), "destroyer" (John 10:10), "roaring lion" (1 Peter 5:8-9), and "murderer" (John 8:44). Each of these titles or descriptive names is related to one basic purpose: destruction. Evil spirits, like Satan, have as their basic purpose the destruction of all that is godly and good in the universe. They are subtle spirits of destruction seeking to eliminate any work of righteousness. A. T. Pierson says:

> *"Evil spirits are continually on the alert to harm both body and spirit—inflict physical evils, and to corrupt intellectual convictions and pervert the heart's affection, and weaken the will—in every way to lead away from truth and God. Their one business is to provoke and promote sinful revolt against the Creator."* [10]

Satan is also referred to in scripture as a "thief" (John 10:10). A thief is one who possesses the characteristic of dishonesty. Such a person cannot be trusted with materials of great value, neither can he be depended upon in any circumstance to guard valuable goods. A thief takes that which does not belong to him. Satan is portrayed in John 10:10 as a stealer of sheep from the

Shepherd's flock. In like manner, evil spirits seek to steal the testimony of Christians. This trait is associated with lying since stealing and lying are both dishonest. The devil is named the "father of lies" and all who are following his leadership are also classified as liars (John 8:44).

One of the most disgusting and despicable traits of satanic beings is deception. Satan is the arch deceiver. He began his deceptive work in the Garden of Eden when he deceived Eve (1 Timothy 2:14). He and his angels have been at their sinister task ever since. Jessie Penn-Lewis records pungent words in her book, War on the Saints, which give insight into the awfulness of deception:

> *"Deceived! How the word repels, and how involuntarily every human being resents it as applied to himself, not knowing that the very repulsion is the work of the deceiver for the purpose of keeping the deceived ones from knowing the truth, and being set free from deception. If men can be so easily deceived by the deception arising from their own fallen nature, how eagerly will the forces of Satan seek to add to it and not diminish it by one iota. How keenly will they work to keep men in bondage to the old creation, out of which spring multitudinous forms of selfdeception, enabling them the more readily to carry on their deceiving work."* [11]

Like Satan, demons are spirits of deception. Deception is one of their most dangerous characteristics. Because of this particular trait, they are of great worth to Satan as he seeks to accomplish his purpose. The Bible mentions at least four types of demons. These are distinguishable by category: (1) The "familiar spirit" is the demon that imitates departed spirits of men (Leviticus 20:6; I Samuel 18:8-10). (2) The "unclean spirit" is the demon that is characterized by impurity (Mark 1:27). (3) Then, as previously determined, the "evil spirits" are known by their trait of wickedness (Luke 7:21). (4) The last of the four types is the "seducing spirit," who has as his distinctive mark the ability to deceive (I Timothy 4:1).

When the scripture gives descriptive and determinative names to demons, it promotes the idea that spirits major in a particular type of evil. Consequently, the "seducing spirit" is more apt at deception than any other type of evil spirit.

SUMMARY

The Bible has revealed demons as personal beings who have the ability to take visible form under certain conditions. They are intelligent beings, having all the faculties of the mind at a superhuman level. The number of evil spirits is not given in scripture, but the fact that they are many is evidenced by such terms as "legion," "hosts," and "powers." This numerous body is part of a vast Satanic kingdom. Demons are exposed as rebellious, dishonest, destructive, deceptive, impure and wicked. Their moral nature is in opposition to God and man.

Jessie Penn-Lewis portrays demons in a rage of uncontrolled wickedness. Speaking of their moral corruption, she says, "When evil spirits act in a rage, they act as a combination to the maddest and most wicked persons in existence, but all their evil is done with fullest intelligence and purpose." [12]

STUDY QUESTIONS

Chapter 4

1. Where did evil spirits come from?

2. Are demons and evil spirits the same?

3. What indicates that demons are personal beings?

4. What are the four types of evil spirits?

NOTES

Chapter 4

1 Edward M. Bounds, Satan: His Personality, Power and Overthrow (Grand Rapids: Baker Book House, 1966) p. 20

2 Ibid., p. 21

3 Merrill F. Unger, Biblical Demonology (Wheaton: Scripture Press, 1967) p.

4 Ibid., p. 64

5 Opinion expressed by Stanley Troussaint in an address Demonism (Tapes for Christ, Dallas, Texas, N.D.)

6 Augustus H. Strong, Systematic Theology (Philadelphia: Judson Press, 1945)p. 450

7 Ibid., p. 445

8 Unger, op. cit., p. 67

9 W. E. Vine, Dictionary of New Testament Words (Westwood, N.J.: F. H. Revell Co., 1966) p. 34

10 A. T. Pierson, The Bible and Spiritual Life (Fincastle, Va.: Scripture Truth Book Co. 1968) p. 175

11 Jessie Penn-Lewis, War on the Saints (Fort Washington, Pa.: The Christian Literature Crusade, N.D.) p. 8

12 Ibid., p. 28

Chapter V

THE POWER OF EVIL SPIRITS

The Bible proclaims that Satan is a powerful being. He is so powerful that he has authority over death. How do we know he has this power? Because, in Hebrews 2:14 the Bible says: "Forasmuch then as the children are partakers of flesh and blood, he also himself likewise took part of the same; that through death he might destroy him that had the power of death, that is, the devil." Satan has the power of death but Jesus has effectively destroyed his power over death by His resurrection.

Any personality who has power over death has superhuman ability. When contemplating power, several questions come to mind: (1) What is power? (2) To what extent is Satan's power limited? (3) To what extent do evil spirits share in Satan's power? In the verse cited above (Hebrews 2:14), the Greek word "kratos" translated "power" means "strength."[1] The word indicates that both force and strength are equal aspects of "power."[2] According to the testimony of God's Word, Satan's power is a significant force in our world. Writing of Christ's assessment of Satan's strength, Bounds says, ". . . instead of minimizing the power of the devil, Jesus exalts him to the pinnacle of power as a prince, with this world as his princedom."[3]

The power of the wicked one is seen in the wilderness as he tempted the Lord Jesus. In one of Satan's three-pronged attacks on our Lord, he offered Christ the kingdom of the whole world. All Christ had to do is worship him (Luke 4:5-8).

Satan claimed that he had the right to offer the world, and Christ did not dispute his claim. Surely Jesus would have challenged Satan's claim had it not been a valid offer. Satan's power was and is extensive, but Satan and his kingdom are not omnipotent. He is limited in his power by the direct will of God. Satan's limitation of power is shown in an incident that took place in man's early history.

The angels came into God's presence to give an account of their activity (Job 1:6-12). God praised His earthly servant Job and Satan responded cynically with an accusation. Satan accused Job of serving God for what he could get out of Him. To prove Job's faithfulness, God allowed Satan to use his power of evil oppression against Job but with definite limitations. God said Satan could not harm Job's physical body (Job 1:12). Satan's power was specifically limited by Jehovah. (For your personal encouragement, you may wish to read the first several chapters of Job for the full story.)

The power of demons is diverse! But, what we want to know is: "How and to what extent can evil spirits affect us in these modern times?" Let's address this question while renewing our commitment to God's Word as our final authority.

POWER TO POSSESS

The ability to possess a human body is the first glaring example of demonic power. Many passages prove that this was true in the days of our Lord. In the writer's opinion, the most arresting example is found in the case of the Gadarene (Mark 5:1-13).[4] We learn several things about demons from the passage. It is quite evident that evil spirits were in complete control of the man's body.

The demons so completely dominated his person that he appeared to be insane. Jessie Penn-Lewis, a popular Bible teacher from England, says of the Gadarene, "His own personality was so mastered by the malignant spirits in possession as to cause him to lose all sense of decency and self-control in the presence of others."[5] The one possessed in this case was so utterly taken over that his own personality was not discernible.

Demonic Vocalization

The passage cited above also reveals that evil spirits can speak by using the vocal apparatus of the person they possess (Mark 5:7). The demon's ability to use the voice box of the possessed person may be observed in many other historical references. For example, some missionaries have testified that they have noticed a peculiar fact when evil spirits speak. In most cases the voice is uniquely different from a human voice. And in almost every incidence they do not sound like the person whose voice box they are using.[6] Paul Gupta, president of the Hindustani Bible Institute in India testifies that on one occasion he dealt with an illiterate Indian woman who was possessed of an evil spirit, and while possessed, the demon spoke in English. Her native tongue was Indian.[7] Careful research revealed that the woman had never learned a language other than her own Indian dialect.

Demonic Strength

The passage in Mark 5:1-13 also indicates that demons have superhuman strength (Mark 5:4). The spirit's strength was so powerful that he could not be bound with chains. Even contemporary missionaries have witnessed this extraordinary strength in people who are demonized.

In a personal interview with missionaries from Columbia, South American, a testimony was given regarding the phenomenal strength of those who have been demonized. Margaret and Orland Corwin, who were under the South American Indian Missions, tell of a Colombian who worships an evil spirit and is considered a witch doctor. When this man begins his worship, he opens himself to demonic power by drinking a special brew which gives the effect of drunkenness; he becomes glassy-eyed, wild, and in this state can accomplish physical feats which a normal human cannot perform.[8]

While many of these cases are not rational to the educated and sophisticated mind, they nonetheless must be admitted if we are to accept credible testimony.

Demonic Brutality

Under certain circumstances evil spirits may cause a possessed person to inflict himself with bodily harm. The Gadarene had self-inflicted wounds caused by cutting himself with stones (Mark 5:5). There is no doubt that evil spirits caused this man's dilemma. Another such incident is recorded in Mark 9:17-29:

> *9:17 And one of the multitude answered and said, Master,I have brought unto thee my son, which hath a dumb spirit;*

9:18 And wheresoever he taketh him, he teareth him: and he foameth, and gnasheth with his teeth, and pineth away: and I spake to thy disciples that they should cast him out; and they could not.

9:19 He answereth him, and saith, O faithless generation, how long shall I be with you? How long shall I suffer you? Bring him unto me.

9:20 And they brought him unto him: and when he saw him, straightway the spirit tare him; and he fell on the ground, and wallowed foaming.

9:21 And he asked his father, How long is it ago since this came unto him? And he said, Of a child.

9:22 And ofttimes it hath cast him into the fire, and into the waters, to destroy him: but if thou canst do any thing, have compassion on us, and help us.

9:23 Jesus said unto him, If thou canst believe, all things [are] possible to him that believeth.

9:24 And straightway the father of the child cried out, and said with tears, Lord, I believe; help thou mine unbelief. 9:25 When Jesus saw that the people came running together, he

*rebuked the foul spirit, saying unto him,
[Thou] dumb and deaf spirit, I charge thee,
come out of him, and enter no more into him.*

*9:26 And [the spirit] cried, and rent him sore,
and came out of him: and he was as one
dead; insomuch that many said, He is dead.*

*9:27 But Jesus took him by the hand, and
lifted him up; and he arose.*

*9:28 And when he was come into the house,
his disciples asked him privately, Why could
not we cast him out?*

*9:29 And he said unto them, This kind can
come forth by nothing, but by prayer and
fasting.*

In this case the demon tore the boy, caused him to foam at the mouth, and to gnash his teeth. The demon even caused the boy to lose consciousness. Time and again the scriptures testify that evil spirits have these unusual powers. In regards to the activity of demons through possession, Clarence Larken says, "The Devilish character of demons is seen in the use they make of their victims." Mrs. George C. Needham in her book about angels and demons says, " . . . evil angels experience malevolent pleasures when they can afflict man with disease of distress. So Satan gloats over Job's calamities."9

All cases in which evil spirits take possession of a human body may not be this bizarre (Mark 1:26). Possession is the most radically evil and sinister of all demonic activity. Evil Spirits cause man pain in less dramatic but equally effective ways.

POWER TO INFLICT DISEASE

On some occasions evil spirits bring physical maladies to those whom they oppress. Several events are recorded in the Bible of people who were physically ill due to demon possession. We find a clear case of demonic activity causing physical illness in Luke 13:11-13:

> *13:11 And, behold, there was a woman which had a spirit of infirmity eighteen years, and was bowed together, and could in no wise lift up [herself].*
>
> *13:12 And when Jesus saw her, he called [her to him],and said unto her, Woman, thou art loosed from thine infirmity.*
>
> *13:13 And he laid [his] hands on her: and immediately she was made straight, and glorified God.*

The woman described in this scripture passage had a spirit of infirmity which had possessed her for eighteen years. The spirit had caused the woman's body to bow with deformity. Cora Taylor, a missionary to Brazil, relates an experience she had with demons and their power to inflict bodily illness. In Brazil there are many spiritualists who will cast plagues on anyone for a fee. They hold their sessions of sorcery in the homes of those purchasing their evil services.

A woman who had recently received Christ as her Savior was accused of telling falsehoods about her neighbor. She tried to quiet her accuser by presenting evidence to prove she was not guilty. Nothing this innocent woman said made may difference. The accuser became so angry that she said, "You'll suffer for this, you just see!"

Shortly after the threat, this woman's eight-year-old boy became ill with rheumatic pains in his legs. The father had a terrible fall which hurt his leg, and she developed a fever. When Mrs. Taylor called on them, the young convert told her of the plague that her neighbor had caused. Mrs. Taylor testified that they had prayer, claiming deliverance from the work of the evil spirit; they resisted Satan on the authority of the shed blood of Christ, and the family was delivered from the plague. 10 It is evident that evil spirits do have the power to afflict a person with dumbness (Matthew 9:32-33) or blindness (Matthew 12:22), They may even cause insanity (Luke 8:26-35) and suicidal mania (Mark 9:22).

When Christ confronted the Gadarene only one of the evil spirits spoke (Mark 5:7), yet it is acknowledged that many demons possessed the man's body (Mark 5:9). Why would one demon speak and the others remain silent? Philip Davis, of Nu-Way Missions, believes that evil spirits have rank and varying degrees of strength. He says the highest ranking evil spirit possessing a body will be the one to speak and will have the most influence over the demonized. He related one experience in which a girl possessed of demons was unconscious, yet when she was spoken to, a demon within her would speak. After Davis cast one demon out, another evil spirit manifested himself in the girl's personality until he too had been cast out. Then another evil spirit was discerned and the process continued until a large number had been cast out and the girl set free.[11]

POWER TO OPPRESS

The examination of demon power, up to this point, has been in the realm of their power to possess human bodies. However, at this point we will do well to consider not only the power of evil spirits to possess a body, but their ability to oppress man. "Oppression" is another level of demonic activity in which the person subjected is attacked by evil spirits. The demons launch their attack, depending upon their purpose, at either the mind or the body of the person being aggravated.

The act of "oppression" is distinctly different from that of "possession" In possession the subject is controlled by one or more spirit beings. Therefore, one considers the condition of possession to be far more serious than oppression.

Oppression is none-the-less real. In Acts 10:38 Christ is described as having been anointed by God with the power to heal all who were oppressed of the devil. In that verse the Greek word "katadunasteno" is translated "oppressed." W. E. Vine says, "This word refers to one having power over or exercising power over a person."[12] The word describes the action Satan wants to take with all humanity. William B. Young, director of World Wide Keswick, makes some pertinent remarks in reference to the word "oppressed." He says: "It is evident from the various shades of meaning of the word 'oppress,' in the Greek, that this operation of Satan is working externally as far as the believer is concerned. It is the working of the enemy without, trying to get within."[13]

Another popular Bible teacher, Theodore H. Epp, says: "The word 'oppress' is significant. It means 'to exercise control over' or 'to tyrannize.' The indication is clear that such oppression is not from within: but from without."[14] Acts 10:38 clearly designates the devil as the author of oppression.

The Screwtape Letters, written by C. S. Lewis presents a series of diabolical and fictitious letters written by a senior demon to one of lesser rank. These letters are somewhat humorous, but they present a very real possibility in the work of evil spirits and the oppression of humanity.[15] The type of oppression presented is an attack upon the mind and an attempted control of outward circumstances.

C. S. Lovett, director of Personal Christianity, maintains that this is the way Satan works in an enlightened society.[16] Temptation is a major tool used of evil spirits to oppress the mind. Many scriptures specifically attribute this power to the devil and the angels of darkness (Genesis 3:1-7; Matthew 4:3; John 13:27; Acts 5:3; I Thessalonians 3:5). Merrill F. Unger says, "Assuredly this power of temptation is possessed by Satan's many subordinate evil spirits, through whose instrumentality he accomplishes his nefarious purposes."[17]

Through the centuries demonic powers have been indefatigably at their work. Only God's Son can defeat these beings of darkness and evil.

Oppression may take form in physical circumstances as illustrated in the case of Job (Job 1:6-12; 2:1-8). Job was oppressed physically in diverse ways. Satan was allowed to employ lightning to destroy his shepherds and their sheep (Job 1:16). He used a great force of wind to destroy Job's home and a number of his servants (Job 1:19). Clearly, demonic powers should not be treated lightly. Satan has real power and his only limitation is placed upon him by God.

The devil and his evil spirits also have the power to oppress through the medium of disease (Job 2:7). Job was afflicted with boils which gave him great pain. In Luke 13:11 a woman is described as having a "spirit of infirmity." Some believe this example is the work of demons afflicting a person with a physical dilemma. It is quite evident that evil spirits have oppressive powers that bring pressure upon man in both the physical and psychic realms.

POWER TO VEX

The third level of demonic activity, which is very closely related to "oppression," is known as "obsession." The Bible term which is synonymous with "obsession" is found in Luke 6:18. Notice the word "vexed" in this verse: "And they that were vexed with unclean spirits; and they were healed" (Luke 6:18). Again, notice the same word in another portion of scripture: "There came also a multitude out of the cities round about unto Jerusalem, bringing sick folks, and them which were vexed with unclean spirits: and they were healed every one (Acts 5:16)." The Greek "ochleo" is translated "vexed" in these passages and means "to mob, i.e., to harass."[19] Evil spirits are seeking to harass mankind.

The meaning of the word "vexed" also conveys the idea of a riot. William B. Young says: "What a picture this gives of the viciousness of the attacks of demons! When they put on a campaign of harassment . . . it is with a rioting, mob spirit."[20] A Bible expositor out of Dallas, TX, J. Dwight Pentecost, expressed the opinion that the purpose of demons in obsession was fourfold: to nullify the testimony of Christians, to defeat them spiritually, to destroy their physical health or strength, and to surround them with countless dangers.[21]

STUDY QUESTIONS

Chapter 5

1. What power do evil spirits have?

2. Can demons or evil spirits inflect disease? Is there Biblical evidence of this happening?

3. What is demon possession and how does it manifest itself?

4. What does "The Screwtape Letters," by C. S. Lewis, reveal about demons?

NOTES

Chapter 5

1 Robert Young, Analytical Concordance to the Bible (Grand Rapids: Eerdman Publishing Co., N.D.) p. 766

2 W. E. Vine, Dictionary of New Testament Words (Westwood, N.J.: F. H. Revell Co.,1966) p. 81

3 E. M. Bounds, Satan: His Personality, Power and Overthrow (Grand Rapids: Baker Book House, 1966) p. 81

4 For a historical discussion of this phenomenon see Chapter III of this book.

5 Jessie Penn-Lewis, War on the Saints, (Fort Washington, Pa.: Christian Literature Crusade, N.D.) p. 29

6 Philip Davis, tape recorded testimony (tape supplied by W. D. Kennedy of Greenville, S.C.)

7 Demon Experience in Many Lands (Chicago: Moody Press, 1960) p. 34

8 Statement by Orland and Margaret Corwin, personal interview (August, 1968).

9 Mrs. George C. Needham, Angels and Demons (Chicago: N.D.) p.79

10 op. cit., Demon Experiences in Many Lands, pp. 120-121

11 Opinion expressed by Philip Davis in a question and answer session ("The Subject of Evil Spirits") (Tape supplied by W. D. Kennedy of Greenville SC: N.D.)

12 Vine, op. cit., p. 143

13 William B. Young, Demon Activity (Goldenrod, Fla.: World-Wide Keswick, N.C.) p. 4

14 Theodore H. Epp, How to Resist Satan (Lincoln, Nebr.: Good News Broadcasting Associations, Inc., 1965) p. 45

15 C. S. Lewis, The Screwtape Letters (NewYork: The McMillian Co., 1966) p.xii

16 C. S. Lovett, Dealing with the Devil (Baldwin Park, California: Personal Christianity, 1967) p.34

17 Merrill F. Unger, Biblical Demonology (Wheaton; Ill., Scripture Press,1967) p. 69

18 Vine, op. cit., p. 186

19 William B. Young, op. cit., p. 7

20 Opinion expressed by J. Dwight Pentecost in a message, ("Satan") (Tapes for Christ, Inc., Dallas, Texas, N.D.).

Chapter VI

SUPERNATURAL OCCULT MANIFESTATIONS OF EVIL SPIRITS

The word "supernatural," in the chapter title, refers to activity beyond the natural experiences of life. The occult arts include: fortune-telling, mind reading, magic, astrology, divining, spiritism, necromancy, and witchcraft. In the last several decades occult activity has been conspicuously obvious. Records indicate a marked increase in every part of the civilized world.

The arts and entertainment world is particularly influenced by the occult and "new age" philosophy. Therefore, we have two questions we need answered: (1)

To what degree do evil spirits affect the occult world? (2) From a theological viewpoint, are evil spirits responsible for occultism? As it is used here, occultism has reference to supernatural agencies and their effect upon mankind. Let us now consider some of the major divisions of the occult arts.

ASTROLOGY

One of the most popular areas of the occult in existence today is astrology, the best known application is the "horoscope." In 1969 Dr. Russell Hitt, Editor of "Eternity," said that more than twelve hundred daily newspapers in America published horoscope columns as compared with only one hundred papers in 1949.[1] It has been estimated that five million people in the United States are devotees of astrology.[2] Astrology is considered by Jan Van Baalen to be a religious cult. He concludes:

> *"Astrology is of a quasi-religious, pagan, idolatrous origin. The Babylonians divided the zodiac into three sections, which were controlled by their chief gods. What happened on earth was a counterpart of that which occurred in heaven. The Greeks knew of a larger number of planets and placed these under the controlling power of their idols, Neptune, Venus, Mars, etc. Each of these gods was supposed to manipulate his planet to further his own interest."[3]*

Dr. Hitt says that the Chaldeans originated the science of astrology and the Greeks and Romans popularized it.[4] It seems that the United States is obsessed with this subject.

Articles about astrology have appeared in periodicals, such as Time, The National Observer, and The New York Times Sunday Magazine. The articles were probably published for no purpose other than to meet public demand. Few people realize that astrology and horoscopes are condemned in scripture. Two passages are of particular significance. Notice in Deuteronomy 17:2-5:

> *17:2 If there be found among you, within any of thy gates which the LORD thy God giveth thee, man or woman, that hath wrought wickedness in the sight of the LORD thy God, in transgressing his covenant,*

> *17:3 And hath gone and served other gods, and worshipped them, either the sun, or moon, or any of the host of heaven, which I have not commanded;*

> *17:4 And it be told thee, and thou hast heard [of it], and inquired diligently, and, behold, [it be] true, [and] the thing certain, [that] such abomination is wrought in Israel:*

> *17:5 Then shalt thou bring forth that man or that woman, which have committed that wicked thing, unto thy gates, [even] that man*

or that woman, and shalt stone them with stones, till they die.

Note also in Isaiah 47:13-14:

47:13 Thou art wearied in the multitude of thy counsels. Let now the astrologers, the stargazers, the monthly prognosticators, stand up, and save thee from [these things] that shall come upon thee.

47:14 Behold, they shall be as stubble; the fire shall burn them; they shall not deliver themselves from the power of the flame: [there shall] not [be] a coal to warm at, [nor] fire to sit before it.

The terms used in these passages refer to the reality of practitioners in astrological arts which God severely condemned. God condemns the worship of "either sun or moon, or any of the host of heaven . . . " (Deuteronomy 17:3). Those who were caught in such practices were to be judged and stoned to death (Deuteronomy 17:5). The severity of God's punishment points to the seriousness of the crime.

An American who wrote a textbook on astrology openly confessed that he went to the roof of his house every noon to worship the sun.[5] Worship of heavenly bodies exists today! God was quite plain about the matter when He inspired Isaiah to designate the various types of soothsayers (fortunetellers). Isaiah designated them as "astrologers," "stargazers," and "monthly prognosticators" (Isaiah 47:13). These too were condemned, and Isaiah foretold their future judgement as revealed by God.

Bill Gothard, director of the Institute of Life Principles, believes that demonic powers are active in astrology.[6] The Bible clearly equates astrology with idol worship and apostasy from the living God. Paul warns about the worship of idols because these ornaments are instruments inspired by evil spirits (1Corinthians 10:20).

Evil spirits use astrology to bring their purpose to pass through the power of suggestion. Dr. Kurt Koch, renowned Lutheran pastor and evangelist who is best known for his research in occult activity, offers the following example.

A minister who saw his mission as fighting superstition had a horoscope cast for the sake of study. He wanted to prove that those casting horoscopes were just practicing a superstitious activity. He really did not believe there was a supernatural element of evil associated with it. He thought that those who trafficked in such things were just in it for greed. Therefore, he set out to prove the industry to be fraudulent. He had to pay a size-able fee because he ordered a detailed personal horoscope cast specifically for him.

He now waited confidently, believing that the horoscope would not fulfill itself. But he was amazed to see that the prophecies were fulfilled. For eight years he observed that all the predictions came true even to the smallest details. He grew uneasy at this and reflected on the problem. It had been his preconceived idea that all occult activity was based on suggestion and superstition. Yet he knew that as a Christian he had not been the victim of suggestion.

Finally he saw no other way of escape than to repent and to ask God for His protection. The thought came to him that he had sinned through this experiment, and had placed himself under the influence of the powers of darkness. After his repentance he discovered that his horoscope was now no longer accurate. Through this experience the minister clearly understood that demonic powers can be active in astrology. The person who exposes himself to this danger can perish by it.[7]

FORTUNE-TELLING

Other means of fortune-telling may be grouped together because their purpose is essentially the same as those described above. Some of the methods which can be put in this category are: cartomancy or fortune-telling through the medium of cards; palmistry or palm reading; divining or the use of tokens to determine good or evil luck. These are only a few of the various types of methods used in telling one of future events. A popular instrument for fortune-telling used by teenagers and children is the Ouija Board. The board as an instrument is often the center of interest at parties and overnight pajama sessions.

Concerning the Ouija Board Bill Gothard says, "The destructive potential of this practice, in addition to giving contra-scriptural guidance, is that it can all too easily plant in the mind detailed predictions or guidance for the future, thus making it as dangerous as fortune-telling."[8]

Evil spirits seem to use fortune-telling to bring their sinister purposes to pass through the power of suggestion. A shocking example of this is given in the following event which took place during World War II:

> *"A young German woman whose husband was missing on the Eastern front went to a card-layer to learn whether her husband was still alive. The soothsayer replied, your husband is dead. The young wife waited three months and again visited a card-layer trying to learn something about the fate of her husband. The fortune-teller responded by saying: 'Your husband will not return.' She went home in despair and turning on the gas killed herself and her two children. The next day the husband returned from the Russian war prison and found the three bodies of his dear ones."[9]*

It is evident in this case that the pseudo or false knowledge obtained from the card-layer so depressed the young mother that she became hopelessly overwhelmed with despair. Similar tragedies occur throughout the world. While we must admit not all of these incidences are demonically energized, there can be no doubt that a good number are.

Another situation was reported to have occurred near Orlando, Florida. Two young schoolteachers were very close friends. One was married and the other was engaged to be married. One evening they decided to go to the county fair. With a festive spirit, they went into a fortune- teller's booth. The fortune-teller spoke to them separately. She spoke first to the engaged girl, then to the other young lady. When the latter was in the booth, she was warned to watch closely over her friend because she said she was going to commit suicide. The fortune-teller was very serious. When the married woman stepped out of the booth, the unmarried girl related to her that the fortune- teller had told her that she was going to commit suicide. The single girl seemed to think it all quite a joke because she could not imagine herself taking such drastic action.

Several days passed and the young married woman missed her friend. She made several attempts to contact her. None were successful. She called her friend's parents, who lived in another state, to inquire about her welfare. They had not heard from her. Finally, as a last resort, she persuaded the landlord to open the apartment in which her friend lived. They found the young woman's body. She had killed herself. It was later discovered that she had broken off her engagement just prior to the carnival outing.[10]

It is impossible for anyone except God to know the direct cause of this girl's death. However, knowing the characteristics and the purpose of evil spirits, one would have to acknowledge that demons were likely (to some degree) active in this incident. Fortune telling, regardless of the form it takes, is condemned by God (Leviticus 20:6). Dr. Koch says, "God is the source of all true prophecies, while the devil is the source of fortune-telling. Prophecy is inspired by the Holy Spirit, but fortune telling is of demonic inspiration."[11]

MAGIC AND WITCHCRAFT

The next major area of investigation is magic. Magic is an elusive term to define. For our purposes, magic will be considered synonymous with witchcraft. Witchcraft involves the activity of magicians, sorcerers, and mediums. (We are not addressing magic as entertainment, but rather the form that traffics in the supernatural.) Biblical references abound which depict God's attitude toward magical arts of a supernatural nature.

The New Testament records the account of a man who so completely bewitched the people that they claimed he had the power of God. This record is found in Acts 8:9-11:

> *8:9 But there was a certain man, called Simon, which before time in the same city used sorcery, and bewitched the people of Samaria, giving out that himself was some great one:*

8:10 To whom they all gave heed, from the least to the greatest, saying, This man is the great power of God.

8:11 And to him they had regard, because that of long time he had bewitched them with sorceries.

The account, as it relates to evil spirits, hinges upon the terms "sorcery" and "bewitched." The word "sorcery" means literally "to practice magic." The Greek word "magos" and our "magic" are derived from it.[12] This exhibition was not natural magic but was supernatural as the word connotes.

The word "bewitched" had reference to the ability of a person to cast a hypnotic spell.[13] Simon literally had the people of Samaria under a spell similar to that of a trance. Then came Philip, preaching the gospel of Jesus Christ, and the people began to believe and to be baptized (Acts 8:12). Simon also believed and was baptized. He continued with Phillip, but when he observed the spiritual power given by the laying on of hands, he offered to purchase this unusual ability. It is evident that he saw the power of God as just a more potent magic than his own. He therefore, coveted it and sought to purchase it thereby showing his true nature (Acts 8:13-19).

The activity of demonic forces is clearly ascertained in the magic of Simon. One may compare his sorcery to that of the magicians in Pharaoh's court (Exodus

7:10-12). The manifestations of Simon's demonic power in Samaria were twofold: (1) he performed supernatural feats which arrested the attention of the people, and (2) he passed himself off as having been one from God. In this way he counterfeited the power of God.[14] One must not make the mistake of counting this incident a natural event. Simon did have supernatural power, but the power did not have God as its source.[15]

Magic and witchcraft still exist today, probably to a greater extent than one realizes. In 1968 England, it was reported that the Witchcraft Research Association claimed a membership of more than eight thousand.[16] The work of this association includes the casting of detailed horoscopes and preparing props for other types of fortune-telling. The members use black magic, which is the casting of spells and plagues upon one's enemies and the use of enchantments and charms to heal. White magic, which is nothing more than black magic in religious garb, is also employed.

In Jamaica and Haiti, Voodoo, a type of black magic, is still flourishing. This magic makes extensive use of some form of fetish. A number of symbolic objects are used in worshiping demons and accomplishing the evil action.[17] Among some groups of our nation, superstition and black magic are common.

A woman told me about her daughter who had married a man whose mother was resentful about the marriage. The mother had not wanted her son to marry. After a short passage of time, jealousy developed between the mother and the daughter-in-law. They were vying for the attention of the young man.

Suddenly and very strangely, the young bride noticed a swelling in her right hand. She was taken to a physician, but after several visits he told her that he could not help her. It was at this stage that the mother of the girl suspected the use of black magic, or Voodoo, as it is known. In fact, the doctor thought of Voodoo also, for he had failed to treat successfully others who had been under a magical spell.

The doctor suggested that the girl be taken to a "head doctor." This term was used to describe a witch doctor who lived in a nearby town. The girl was taken, and after a fee had been agreed upon the spell was cast off. Within hours the hand was normal again. It was discovered later that the mother-in-law had placed the spell upon the girl by getting her to eat, without her knowledge, a specially prepared magical potion.[18]

Indicators suggest that occult magic is common in the United States. It is common to find people in almost every town or village who can talk off warts, talk the fire out of burns, and remove rash from babies' mouths. The ability to perform such feats is commonly known as white magic and is sometimes mixed with religious beliefs. Many even think of it as a gift from God. However, in each case the healing is subject to particular enchantments, magical formulas, and quoting of Bible verses. In some situations the three highest names are used: the "Father," the "Son," and the "Holy Ghost."

Regardless of how often the names of the "Trinity" are used, it is nothing more than a formula for activating the power of white magic and it is not of God. Dr. Koch says, "In true prayer God is involved. The white magician is inspired by the powers of darkness."[19]

One afternoon I was making a pastoral call and we were seated on the front porch. During our conversation, a car drove into the yard. One of the persons in the car called for the lady of the home. She went to the car and discovered that a teenage boy had been badly burned. She took the burned limb in her hands. She repeated an incantation under her breath, moved one hand in a circle over the burn, and then blew on it. She repeated this several times, and the pain the lad was suffering left him.

The church member later related the fact that she had used a Bible verse and also the name of the "Trinity" in the healing. This formula was passed down to her from a male relative.[20] This may seem to be a harmless power, but it aids the powers of darkness and dishonors the God of the universe.

God is dishonored because the healing is not a result of faith in what God has done, but rather in the recitation of a magical formula. The above process is nothing more than a fulfillment of demonically inspired supernatural activity. All of the supernatural manifestations are the same in character. Astrology and fortune telling are essentially the same. Satan uses different means to arrive at the same end. Magic, or witchcraft, while having a different purpose, stems from the same source of power as fortune telling.

SPIRITISM

Spiritism is the final division of supernatural manifestations to be considered. It is probably the most weird and dangerous of all the areas covered. Spiritism is a religion, yet it is considered by some adherents to be a union with Satan. When we studied the history of Saul's visit to a spiritist (in Chapter II), we discussed the most obvious reference to spiritism in the Bible (I Samuel 28:7-14).

Spiritism is the alleged act of communication with the dead. The Bible does not recognize the existence of legitimate spiritism. It does, however, recognize the fact that people exist who claim to be channels for spirits (Deuteronomy 18:11).

I know of no record that will allow a person to accurately estimate the age of spiritism. It seems to have existed in some form in every generation since the curse of Cain. Basically, the spiritist works in a seance where one person acts as a medium through whom the supposed spirit of a deceased person communicates with the other persons in the room. The means of communication are varied. In some instances, the spirit speaks, using the voice of the medium, or speaks out of midair. On other occasions, the spirit may have the medium write, or he may appear in an apparition or ghost-like form. He may also use rapping to communicate messages through a code which the participants have previously agreed upon with the spiritist.

Do supernatural powers actually exist in the area of spiritism? Jan Van Baalen writes: "Spiritists who have gone into the matter deeply have occasionally confessed to obsession by vile and evil spirits. E. F. Hanson's excellent book contains several pages filled with quotations from such spiritist authorities as the magazine 'Mind and Matter' in which it is admitted that mediums are at times subject to the control of evil spirits . . . " In support of this quote is the testimony of mediumistic or psychic people who, after a few experiments, discarded spiritism entirely because the information they received was so unspeakably vile, obscene, and blasphemous that they were fairly shocked out of spiritism.[21]

John L. Nevis says of spiritism, "I believe it to be but another name for demon possession."[22] No doubt much of the so-called spiritism is a hoax, but one can be deceived by those who are fraudulent. Anyone who toys with spiritism (even when pretending) can become a tool of Satan. Spiritism does have supernatural aspects. This fact is illustrated by the following two accounts.

Evil Spirits using Objects as Mediums

Robert Kraus, a freelance newspaper writer, reported an unusual story which had been authenticated by at least one hundred witnesses. The story's dateline was

Newberry, Michigan, the hometown of Roger Nisbet, a marine who had been killed in Vietnam. Roger's personal effects were sent home to his family. A ring was among the articles. Roger's older brother began wearing the ring. Shortly after a grave side ceremony, the older brother, Bill Nesbit, was drinking coffee with his wife when she was startled by a strange brown thread protruding out of the top of the ring. Soon the threads started coming out in various colors and shapes. They would spell out words by forming letters. The word "love" was formed and an outline of Vietnam appeared.

The local priest expressed the opinion that Roger's spirit, using the ring as a medium, was seeking to communicate with the family. After the threads began to appear, strange noises and movements were observed in the Nisbet home. They heard pounding on the downstairs door, but no one was there. On one occasion, friends were visiting the family in the living room when a crash was heard upstairs. An investigation revealed that Roger's flag had mysteriously toppled onto the floor against all laws of gravity. On another occasion, Mr. Nisbet, the father, was awakened by something thrown over his head. It was his own jacket which he had hung in the hallway.[23] These people were convinced that an element of the supernatural was involved.

Mediums in Occult Activity

Another rather unusual event involving the supernatural was reported by Diane Pike, widow of the late, controversial Episcopal bishop, James A. Pike. She told of her experiences during the search for her husband, who was lost in a barren canyon near Bethlehem. She had been with him, but had left to search for help. When she returned, Dr. Pike was nowhere to be found. An extensive search ensued.

During this search, she described herself as having begun a constant prayer which, she said, opened the way for Pike to draw strength from her. She placed a call to Arthur Ford, an American spiritist who had assisted Pike in allegedly communicating with his deceased son. Ford forwarded a message to her that he had a vision of Jim Pike in a cave near the place she had left him.

Later a message came from Edna Twigg. Mrs. Twigg was the British medium with whom Pike had first sought to communicate with his son. This Medium told Mrs. Pike that her husband was probably already on the other side because she had some communication from him, but it had been a confusing session. Then other information came from an Israeli medium saying that Pike had not been found because of overhanging bushes.

This medium also said that Pike was unconscious and they would have to hurry. Another day's search revealed nothing as to the location of Pike. That evening Mrs. Pike had a vision of a husky old woman dressed in a white robe, holding a large candle. She interpreted this vision as the coming of death. She resisted the vision, and it vanished. She then began to concentrate harder to give her husband strength.

She fell asleep. About 3:30 A.M. she was startled awake. She heard voices talking about her husband dying. A vision came into focus; she could see her husband's body, the position in which it was lying, the general location of the body, and other details. She reported that she saw her husband's spirit leave his body and ascend into heaven. She watched as her husband's spirit was being received by a host of spirits that had gone on before him. Among these spirits she named Jim Pike, Jr., Bobby Kennedy, and Paul Tillich. She shared this vision as it took place with her younger brother.

After the vision, the younger brother requested his sister to draw a picture of what she had seen in the vision concerning the location of Pike's body. She drew the picture. The next morning, Bishop Pike's body was discovered. Mrs. Pike stated:

> *"My vision that Sunday morning actually reflected rather closely the circumstances in which they found Jim's body. There were distortions, of course, but the "picture" was amazingly accurate."*[24]

These experiences show the reality of the supernatural in the lives of people living in our era. I admit that some of the reports could be exaggerated.

However, these events relate closely to the findings reported by reputable investigators.

Numerous accounts are available in books written by Kurt E. Koch and John L. Nevis which substantiate the fact that evil supernatural personalities have the power to produce the results described in the incidents cited above. Again, I want to make it very clear that the Bible recognizes evil spirits as the energizing source behind the occult activities of our world.

STUDY QUESTIONS

Chapter 6

1. How is astrology related to the supernatural?

2. How do demons influence fortune telling?

3. How are demons involved in the occult?

4. What is the difference in "white" and "black" magic?

END NOTES
CHAPTER 6

1 Russell T. Hitt, Demons Today, Eternity XX (May, 1969) p. 9

2 Jan karel Van Baalen, The Chaos of Cults (Grand Rapids: Eerdman Publishing Co., 1960), p. 20

3 Ibid., p. 28

4 Hitt, op. cit., p. 9

5 Van Baalen, op. cit., p. 28

6 Opinion expressed by Bill Gothard in a lecture at Keswick, N.J. (January,1969)

7 Kurt E. Koch, Between Christ and Satan (Grand Rapids: Kregel Publications,1967) p. 17

8 Gothard, op. cit., opinion expressed.

9 Kurt E. Koch, Christian Counseling and Occultism (Grand Rapids: Kregel Publications, 1965) p. 67

10 Statement by Dan Wilson, personal interview (September, 1969). (He is related to one of the parties in the case cited.)

11 Kurt E. Koch, Between Christ and Satan, p. 50

12 Charles J. Elliot (ed.) Commentary on the Whole Bible (Grand Rapids: Zondervan Publishing Co., 1959) Vol. VII, p. 48

13 Ibid., p. 48

14 Opinion expressed by J. Dwight Pentecost in a message (Trafficking with Demons) (Tapes for Christ, Dallas, Texas)

15 David Thomas, Acts of the Apostles (Grand Rapids; Baker Book House, 1955),p. 117

16 Ray S. Buker, Sr., Are Demons Real Today, Christian Life, XXIX (March, 1968) p. 42

17 Opinion expressed by Charles Piepgrass in a lecture, (Demonism) (Tapes for Christ, Dallas, Texas, N.C.)

18 Statement by Pauline Coleman, personal interview (October, 1968).

19 Koch, Between Christ and Satan, p. 76

20 A personal pastoral experience of the writer.

21 Van Baalen, op. cit., p. 49

22 John L. Nevis, Demon Possession (Grand Rapids: Kregel Publications, 1968)p. 323

23 Robert Kraux, The Ring, The Charlotte Observer, January 6, 1970, p. 4B

24 Diane Kennedy Pike, Bishop Ike's Triumph Over Death, Ladies Home Journal, LXXVII (February, 1970, p. 71

Chapter VII

THE PHENOMENA OF EVIL POSSESSION

At this point in the study of evil spirits, the following questions arise: (1) Does geography have any relationship to the phenomenon of demon possession? (2) What are the degrees of possession? (3) What are the limitations of possession? (4) What are the stages of possession? (5) What is the means of defeating evil spirits?

The quest for information is often extra biblical. Therefore, we must delve into the findings of missionaries, doctors, counselors, and ministers. Only those who have had valid experiences, tested by biblical principles, will be considered. Admittedly, at this point,

115

one must rest heavily upon the spiritual insight and Christian reputations of those reporting.

GEOGRAPHICAL FREEDOM

The possession of people by evil spirits seems to have no geographical boundaries. In Europe, Dr. Koch has ably gathered hundreds of documented cases of people who have suffered from possession by evil spirits. In China, during the nineteenth century, Dr. Nevis researched demonic activity and wrote a paper presenting his discoveries. He found that demonic activity, about which he had previously been skeptical, was a dreaded reality among the Chinese. He substantiated his findings by collaborating with other Christian workers who had already had similar experiences. His book, which may now be out of print, is probably the most valuable of all the works I consulted on the subject.

From India come reports of deep-seated demonism among the Hindus.[1] Dr. Ray Buker, professor of missions at the Conservative Baptist Theological Seminary, reports that his son had encountered demon possession in West Pakistan.[2] In the Caribbean, demon possession also abounds. Haiti is particularly infested.[3] Likewise, the whole of South America is alive with cases of demonic possession. Reports on the activity of evil spirits in South America have come from numerous sources.

In the United States, demon possession is not commonly acknowledged outside of a Christian context. The reality of supernatural personal beings influencing humans is not commonly accepted. At least it is not recognized as such, possibly because of the influence of philosophical rationalism upon the western mind. Psychiatry, to my knowledge, does not recognize the existence of supernatural spirits. However, Carl Taylor, a missionary to Brazil, states that he knows a Christian psychiatrist who believes that every schizophrenic case is actually demonomania.[4] Many incidences in which evil spirits actually possess people have been recorded in the United States and Canada.

AN INCIDENT IN CHICAGO

The writer had occasion to personally interview Danny Kennedy, a Bible college student, who had experience with evil spirits[5] This case was checked for accuracy with the testimony of a German student who witnessed the event. [6] These students were attending a seminar in Chicago in late August, 1968, and it was during one of the seminar's sessions that the demonized was encountered. This case revolved around a young man whom we will call Jim. He was rather unusual in that he was offensive and those attending the seminar were not eager to socialize with him. He exhibited resentment and an attitude which was characterized by pride and arrogance. His discussions regarding Bible truths were distorted because he sought to spiritualize everything about Bible truths.

117

On the last evening of the conference, a film was shown about the life of John Wesley. In this film a scene was viewed in which an unauthorized Christian took charge of a worship service. John Wesley was portrayed as chiding the young man. In this period of history, no one was to preach except ordained ministers. As a minister of the Church of England, John Wesley agreed with this position. Wesley's mother defended the would be preacher. During the scene, Jim stood up and said, "Father, rebuke her." He appeared to stagger and would not be seated. Several men drew him aside and quieted him until the film ended.

It seemed that Jim had identified himself with the uneducated man who had preached. Jim wanted to attend a certain school but lacked the educational background; this was the source of his resentment. The director of the seminar began asking Jim questions. He asked Jim if he had any dealings with the devil. Jim replied with irrelevant spiritual discourses.

Danny Kennedy was sitting behind Jim and suspected that he was possessed with a demon. Danny prayed and asked the Lord if his suspicion was true to confirm it. Jim began to shake as if in convulsions. Danny leaned forward and said, "Demon, in the name of Christ, speak and give your name." Immediately, a voice that was not Jim's answered, "Lucifer." Danny commanded "Lucifer" to come out. Jim's throat swelled and he coughed. At Danny's order a second demon gave his name as "Beelzebub." Danny also commanded "Beelzebub" to come out.

Then Jim stood up and shouted, "I'm free; I'm free!" Again he began talking in an irrelevant manner about spiritual things. Danny discerned that a demon was talking, not Jim. Therefore, Danny challenged him saying, "You are a liar; you have not come out yet; how many of you are in Jim?" Again a demon answered, indicating that thousands of evil spirits were possessing the man. Danny asked for the truth and the demon gave seven as the real number. Danny testified that the demons lied about a number of things. These demons were stubborn and would not be cast out. During this time other men and women attending the seminar were praying, claiming the promises of God by quoting scripture verses, and singing softly songs about the blood of Christ. Those reporting on the occasion said it was amazing what a oneness of mind prevailed.

One of the ministers present approached Jim, who was in a semiconscious state on the floor, and asked, "Jim, can you hear me?" Jim answered that he could and sat up. The minister began talking to Jim about sin and submission in his life. Claiming that a Jew could not confess to gentiles, Jim resisted this discussion. He was reminded by the minister that in Christ all were one. Jim then confessed that his problem was pride; he said he had an impulsive desire to be like God, to actually take God's place. He further confessed that if it took demons to accomplish this purpose, he wanted the evil spirits. He also said he wanted to be like John Wesley, possessing the power Wesley when he spoke. Danny Kennedy expressed the opinion that the demons would not leave Jim because he had subjected himself to the evil spirits.

The minister talked to Jim about Jesus Christ and his need for salvation. Jim then made a definite commitment Demon Possession to God and subjected himself to the Lordship of Christ as his personal Savior. After this commitment, Jim denounced Satan and his evil spirits. Danny said, "Jim, let's get rid of the demons." Jim agreed. Danny then commanded the demon in Christ's name to acknowledge his presence. The demon spoke, saying he was the spirit of pride. Jim's throat began to swell, he started coughing and the demon was exorcized.

This process continued until at least six demons were cast out. These evil spirits identified themselves as pride, impurity, hypocrisy, overriding, anger, and deceit. When the demon of anger manifest himself, Jim's face displayed angry contortions. The demon told Danny that he would like to kill him, but could not because the blood of Christ was covering him. Jim's body began shaking; he went into physical distortions. Danny demanded in the name of Christ that the demon come out; again, the swelling of the throat and the coughing commenced as the demon was expelled.

The demon of deceit was more stubborn and rebellious than all the evil spirits that had been previously confronted. He threatened to come out and possess someone in the room or on the campus. The demon made Jim point to Danny's sister, Pat Kennedy, and threatened her saying, "I'll go into that girl over there." Pat met the demon's threat with the promise of Christ's protection. The people present formed a circle and joined hands. They sang songs about the power of the blood of Christ and the omnipotence of God. Then they prayed, committing the victory to the Lord. This experience lasted from 9:00 P.M. until 4:45 A.M. of the next day.

Several weeks after the seminar, Jim wrote the director asking that he be forgiven for his prideful attitude. No other follow-up information is available concerning this case. The writer personally checked the accuracy of this event and found the case did actually take place. It was the first experience with evil spirits by anyone in attendance. Danny Kennedy had heard the testimonies of missionaries and had only a theoretical knowledge of demonic activity. This example of demon possession in America closely parallels examples in the New Testament.

A CASE IN NEW ORLEANS

Another case of demon possession in the United States relates the reality of evil spirits as they were tormenting a young woman called Jane.[7] The woman lived in New Orleans. She was married and the mother of several young children. She developed symptoms similar to someone who may be considered mentally ill. Some of the symptoms were beating her head against the wall; threatening to kill her children; beating on her breasts and other parts of her body. She often had fits of jerking, throwing herself on the floor and suffering from convulsive seizures. Jane had to be watched day and night. Her husband had spent a great sum of money on psychiatrists to no avail. Declared hopeless, she was sent home from a famous psychiatric clinic. Jane's husband was advised to have her committed to a terminal institution.

As a last resort the husband contacted his pastor for any possible help. The pastor testified that he and a group of people from the church went to Jane's house the next time she had a seizure. The pastor suspected the work of demons and he decided to try Jane's spirit. The pastor commanded the spirit to speak. The spirit tried to remain silent. This silence seemed to be a deceptive move by the demon. After several commands, the demon had to speak because the pastor had made his demands based on Jesus' authority and not his own. He gave his name as "Thadeus." The preacher conversed with the demon, actually aggravating him to get information. The pastor asked the demon if Lucifer was his father; the demon answered that he was. The demon also was asked if he was in existence when Christ was ministering in the world. Again the demon said "Yes." After the preacher had finished gathering sufficient information to prove that evil spirits were present, he started commanding the demon to leave. A tape recorder was used to preserve this session and the sessions that followed. Before the demon was finally cast out, a coughing spell ensued. Then, another demon called "Danius" manifested himself. He too, was cast out. Other demons were likewise exorcized.

The demons were cast out of Jane five times. Each session was shorter than the one before it. Each demon portrayed a different personality. Their voices were distinctly different in either pitch or huskiness, yet Jane's voice box was used. During one of the sessions an evil spirit tried to tempt the preacher. The demon told the preacher to listen to him and he would make him famous.

On another occasion, during the taped session, the demon testified that if Satan had won the battle in the wilderness temptations of Jesus all their troubles would have been over. Jane was freed from the bondage of demons. She and her husband have moved to another state. The preacher was given the opportunity to speak at a seminar for psychiatrists about how he was able to effect her cure. He presented the recordings of the sessions and explained his method for casting out demons.

You are no doubt surprised, as was I, to learn of such unusual cases existing in this nation. The examples offered are similar to others reported from all over the world. Evil spirits are not limited by geographical scope. They apparently are free to roam the earth, vexing, aggravating, oppressing, and possessing whenever their work is not hindered by God.

The illustrations above are shared to show that demonic activity is more common today than is normally acknowledged. **I do not necessarily agree with how the demonized subjects were dealt with and counseled. I**

will address what I believe to be a biblical strategy for our present dispensation in the next chapter.

DEGREES OF POSSESSION

Investigation of the phenomenon of possession presents several major difficulties. One problem is the distinction between the degrees of possession. Is it possible to be more or less possessed? Perhaps a better term would be levels of possession.

Dormant Possession

One discernible degree of possession may be titled "Dormant possession." In this degree the fact that a person is possessed by an evil spirit is not apparent. A Biblical illustration of this degree of possession is observed in Judas Iscariot (Luke 22:3). The Bible refers to Judas as having his heart filled by Satan. Judas' behavior did not indicate to those around him that he was under satanic control. Therefore, his possession was dormant and not obvious to observers. We may also observe in another case the dormant possession of Ananias (Acts 5:3). However, in each of these examples, the person involved was held responsible for his actions, even though the devil was possessing him.

Derek Prince, an Englishman and student of the Bible who now resides in the United States, shares an experience which took place in a worship service he was

124

leading. Dr. Prince was speaking about God's power over Satan. A young woman who played the piano was seated on the front pew. At a particularly strong point in the message, the young woman gave an unearthly scream and slumped to the floor. Dr. Prince said he discerned that it was the work of a demon. He commanded the spirit to speak. The demon gave his name as "lies." This spirit and several other evil spirits were cast out. The congregation was startled. The girl thanked God, quietly but audibly, for her deliverance. This young woman had not shown signs of demonic activity in her life. She was considered by those around her to be a normal person with certain bad habits.[8]

These examples are designated as dormant possession. The outstanding characteristic of this degree of possession is the deceptive appearance of normalcy, yet certain satanic traits are discernible in the personality. The subject maintains his rationale through his possession experience, except when he descends into total possession, as did the young woman in the worship service.

Spasmodic Possession

Another degree of possession is called "spasmodic possession." A biblical example of spasmodic possession is observed in the case of the lad who had convulsive seizures (Matthew 17:14-18). It seems that this child had periodic seizures of possession. In this degree of possession, the person is quite normal until attacked. According to reports available, these attacks last anywhere from a few minutes to days. The attacks are unpredictable in their timing. Only a few samples of cited cases reveal that such attacks do exist. John L. Nevis cites the following record as an account of intermittent possession:

> *"Margaret B. _____ at eleven, of lively disposition, but a godly pious child, was on the nineteenth of January, 1829, without having been previously ill, seized with convulsive attacks, which continued with few and short intermissions for two days. The child remained unconscious so long as the convulsive attacks continued. She rolled her eyes, made grimaces, and performed all kinds of curious movements with her arms... On the forenoon of the twenty-sixth... these attacks ceased... On the thirty-first of January, the same condition returned with the same symptoms . . . At this period the violence of the fury, blasphemy and curses reached their highest degree. . . .On the ninth of February, which, like the twenty-sixth of January . . . this most lamentable trouble came to the end."*[9]

Total Possession

The final degree of possession we will consider is "total possession." In total possession the person is utterly dominated by evil spirits. His own personality is completely hidden. This type of possession very closely resembles the state of mental derangement or insanity. The maniac of Gadara (Matthew 8:28-32) is an example of total possession. In 1868 a Chinese preacher cast the demons out of a native boy who had been possessed for ten or more days. The boy was totally out of character and attacked whoever came near.[10]

Demonic Limitations

The next area to be investigated is the limitations evil spirits have in possession. Only one limitation exists of which the examiner may be sure. That limitation may be stated as the permissive will of God. Evil spirits cannot do anything which God will not allow them to do. Beyond this fact all is debatable. Information is obscure. Revelation is too dark to establish any possibilities in this area.

PROGRESSIVE STAGES OF POSSESSION

A person may go through discernible stages of possession. Records exist which show that possession can be instantaneous. Some records indicate that a definite process of progressive steps was passed through before the subject was completely demonized. We need a concise definition for possession. For the purpose of our investigation, possession is the presence of an evil spirit within a person's body, whether or not the demon is exercising total control over the personality. However, one weakness exists in this definition: how does one know the difference between a demon-influenced and a demon-possessed person? Jessie Penn-Lewis answers the question when she says, "In demon influence people follow their own wills and retain their own personality."[11] If this is true, it follows that there are two ways for a person to know if a demon is possessing him. (1) He knows when he loses all control over his will and personality. (2) He knows he is possessed when he consciously and willingly yields to temptation.

Four stages of progression emerge from these examples: 1) a siege of overbearing temptation; 2) demon influence to the point that a person finds himself obsessed with some evil thought or deed; 3) yielding to impulsive obsessive desires; 4) the evil spirit takes complete control.

These stages are applicable only in situations where definite transitions occur. These stages are the stages of involuntary possession. Voluntary possession, which we will not investigate, is the process one passes through in order to become a medium. The terms "casting out demons" and "exorcizing demons" are not technically the same. Dr. Unger says:

> *"Strictly speaking there are no exorcisms in the Bible. Use of the word, in its essential etymological meaning, forbids its employment with regard to the expulsion of demons by our Lord or His disciples. The word signifying, as it does, the casting out of evil spirits by conjurations, incantations, or religious or magical ceremonies, is singularly appropriate*

to describe Jewish and ethnic practice, but is in salient contrast to that of our Lord and His followers, who employed no such methods."[12]

Demons may be cast out by those who are not Christians (Acts 19:13).[13] However, only one person has ultimate authority over Satan and evil spirits. That person is the Lord Jesus Christ; evil spirits have to leave when commanded by Him. Therefore, the only lasting deliverance from evil spirits is God's Son, Jesus Christ. Lasting results are obtained by continued obedience to Christ. Christ is the victor, and He has the trusting and obedient soul in His care.

Study Questions

1. The author suggests three possible degrees or levels of demon possession. Name them.

2. What are the limitations of demon possession?

3. Name and describe the authors observations about the four possible stages of possession.

NOTES
CHAPTER 7

1 Demon Experiences in Many Lands (Chicago: Moody Press, 1960) pp. 19-38

2 Ray B. Buker, Sr., "Are Demons Real Today", Christian Life, XXIX, (March,1968) p. 43

3 Opinion expressed by Charles Peipgrass in a lecture ("Demonism") (Tapes for Christ, Dallas, Texas, N.D.)

4 Statement by Carl Taylor, recorded interview, (tape supplied by W. D. Kennedy, Greenville, S.C. N.D.)

5 Statement by Danny Kennedy, personal interview, September, 1968.

6 Statement by Dandwart Essbaum, personal interview, September, 1968

7 "Story of Jane," a tape recorded session of demons being cast out of a woman in the city of New Orleans (tape supplied by W. D. Kennedy, Greenville, S.C.)

8 Derek Prince, "Release from Depression",

Christian Life, XXIX, (March, 1968), p. 67

9 John L. Nevis, Demon Possession (Grand Rapids: Kregel Publications, 1968), pp. 122-125

10 Ibid., p. 77

11 Jessie Penn-Lewis, War on the Saints (Fort Washington, Penn.: Christian Literature

Crusade, N.D.), 144

12 Merrill Unger, Biblical Demonology (Wheaton, Ill.: Scripture Press, 1967)p. 101

13 For a discussion of exorcism by those who are not Christian, refer to Chapter III of this book.

Chapter VIII

SPIRITUAL WARFARE AND EVIL SPIRITS

In Chapter I we determined that Satan is the father of evil and that his ultimate purpose is to defeat God. We also learned that evil spirits aid the devil in his work. Considering these facts, we need to know all that can be discovered about evil spirits and their influence upon the Christian and all other members of the human race.

Four specific areas will be investigated: 1) the how of demonic influence, 2) the methods employed, 3) demon possession as it relates to the Christian, and 4) the Christian's defense.

DEMONIC INFLUENCE

Before you become a Christian, demonic powers influence you on three levels. Why three levels? Because, man is made up of three parts. There is biblical evidence that suggests man is made up of spirit, soul and body (I Thessalonians 5:23). A nationally known Bible teacher observes:

> *"The Greek word 'Kai' which is translated 'and' is used between spirit and soul as well as between soul and body. This grammatical construction clearly shows that the spirit differs from the soul and that the soul differs from the body."* [1]

The view above describes man as a trichotomy. Most scholars reject the trichotic (meaning three parts) position in favor of the dichotic (meaning two parts). The dichotomist believes that man is made up of two parts: the material and the immaterial. The trichotomist believes man to be made up of three parts: one physical part (the body), and two immaterial parts (the soul and spirit). We have to admit that in the Old Testament the soul and spirit are often used interchangeably. However, when you analyze the theology of the apostles (particularly Paul) you find strong statements which lead to the conclusion that man may very well be a three-part being.

Man as a three-part being, parallels the nature of God. Biblically, God is a triune God; He is three yet one in essence. God is Spirit and man is spirit. God has a body (His name is Jesus) and man has a body which houses his spirit and soul. God is a conscious, rational, emotional, and volitional being and that part of Him may be referred to as soul. In the same sense man mirrors God and has a soul that is conscious, rational, emotional and volitional. The animal kingdom is different from the human race in that animals have no consciousness of God.

We must never make the above explanation an issue of contention. We must strive to understand those who disagree. If we do not we will fall prey to the very spirits of evil whom we are combating.

When one is not a Christian, the devil has access to each part of his being. However, after one is born from above, Satan no longer has access to his spirit. Evil spirits cannot possess the spirit of the Christian who walks in the Spirit, because, the Holy Spirit has complete possession. However, demons still may vex the soul and body. For an understanding of how demons influence us, we must know the distinctions among the body, the soul, and the spirit.

The spirit of man is his spiritual consciousness. This consciousness enables man to receive spiritual insight and to perceive the essential nature of God. The body is on the other end of the spectrum. The body is the faculty through which man receives information concerning the physical world around him. Man uses his senses (smell, touch, see, hear, and taste) to gather physical information. The soul is the mind or the psychological part of man's being. The mind is where the spirit and body are perfectly united.² The soul make decisions based upon information it receives from the physical and spiritual arenas. The soul is the deciphering mechanism or the information center of man. It is in the soul that man makes his decisions. It is in the soul that action is determined and the will is exercised.

DEMONS INFLUENCE
MIND AND BODY

The mind and body are both vulnerable to attack by evil spirits because the nature of spiritual battle. If possible, the demons seek to obsess, oppress, and possess every human and especially Christians. Their purpose in attacking is to abort the will of God in man and especially the believer's life. In chapter five the power of evil spirits was discussed in reference to the natural elements. It was also shown that they may inflict a person with disease or bodily harm. However, in my opinion, their power over the natural elements and man's body is minor compared to their influence upon man's psyche. The Christian is at war with the forces of darkness. When at war, we are always interested in the methods the enemy will use and in his attack upon believers.

The scriptures make it plain that evil spirits attack believers through our thought processes (Romans 7:23). Demons have access to the mind. C. S. Lovett, Director of Personal Christianity, says, "Satan wants to control our thought life by imposing his own."[3] If evil spirits had the power to completely control the thought life, man would be nothing more than a puppet. God has given man the ability to make choices and the devil can't make us do anything. We are free until we surrender to him a stronghold in our lives by our willful rebellion against God.

Demons make it their business to present enticing thoughts to the mind which, if followed, will lead the Christian into sin. In this relationship, evil spirits have access to the mind, and they seek to control the thought life through the medium of suggestion. Psychologists have proven suggestion to be an extremely powerful tool when dealing with man.

Demons seek to oppress the Christian's mind with anxieties, doubts, cares, worries, troubled thoughts, and tensions. Tension is often the cause of psychosomatic suffering which may be a symptom of being oppressed by evil spirits. Joseph Carroll, Bible teacher and conference speaker, expresses the opinion that fear, grief, and anger are three dangerous emotions. These emotions are dangerous because they give place to the devil if one indulges himself in them.[4] The believer can progress in his indulgence to the point that he becomes bound by Satan. In reference to bondage, Dr. L. Gilbert Little, a psychiatrist, has written the following observation:

"Men and women possessed with fear of fears not only demonstrate that a powerful

*influence has them bound to self, but they
frequently express it in words. As one patient
expressed, 'I am caught in a trap. But how to
get out of it? I can look back and know how I
got there, but it was so gradual, over the
years, that I did not realize my plight until I
was caught. I want to get well. I want help
from you, but something tells me to scream
No! No! When you talk about Jesus.' Another
patient said, 'My head goes around in a
whirl. I am afraid my mind will go blank if I
listen to you.'"⁵*

When the believer gives place to Satan, demons are
free to begin their oppression. The oppression always
hinders the Christian's attempt to make progress in
spiritual study and service. Some of the methods demons
use are discussed by Theodore Epp. He lists: worry,
fretting, complaining, vain imaginations, evil thoughts,
anger, harshness, suspicion, fanaticism, irritableness,
critical spirit, spirit of revenge, fear, grief, contention,
impatience, sensitiveness, pride, frustration, heresy,
conceit, jealousy and many others.⁶ Each of these
methods originates with the impression of thoughts upon
the mind. Evil spirits have the ability to impress the mind
of a person with their thoughts. The impression is often
made in such a manner that the person believes the
thoughts are his own. ⁷

Another method used by demons to retard the
Christian's spiritual growth is temptation. Evil spirits
appeal to the fallen nature in man. They realize each

person's weak points. An example of temptation in a young person's life may be ambition. In this situation, demons may seek to entice the young person to the point that he is obsessed with thoughts of getting ahead. Consequently, his spiritual life is starved. Joseph Carroll says that Satan used ambition to control the lives of unsuspecting Christians.[8] Most Christians are unaware of an attack when these traits are found in their own lives.

INFLUENCE
THROUGH DECEPTION

Deception is the most dangerous of all the methods evil spirits use. Deception is dangerous because it has a more devastating effect as an end result. The Bible gives some very practical advice about how to stand against deception. The believer is commanded to stand "against the wiles of the devil" (Ephesians 6:11). The word "wiles" means deception.

The Bible warns the believer about deception in at least eight areas: 1) the believer is warned about the purpose of Satan to deceive (Matthew 24:24); 2) one is deceived who does not practice the truth he hears (James 1:22); 3) a person is deceived who claims to have no sin (1 John 1:8); 4) a man who thinks more of himself than he ought is deceived (Galatians 6:3); 5) one who thinks he is wise because he has worldly wisdom is deceived (I Corinthians 3:18); 6) a man who claims to be a Christian and does not control his tongue is deceived (James 1:26); 7) the person who does not think he will reap what he sows is deceived (Galatians 6:7); 8) one is deceived who practices sin (I Corinthians 6:9,10).

In each of these areas evil spirits seek to deceive the child of God. Spiritual warfare is difficult because the enemy is not easily discerned. The enemy has a super-intelligence network and he is capable of counterfeiting every work that God performs in the believer. He seeks to counterfeit spiritual relationships giving the impression of acceptance with God. These counterfeits become effectual only when the believer falls for them.

Jessie Penn-Lewis's words, showing her perception about evil spirits, are worthy of our consideration:

> *"Deceiving spirits carefully adapt their*
> *suggestions and leadings to the idiosyncrasies*
> *of the believer, so that they do not get found*
> *out; i.e., no 'leading' will be suggested*
> *contrary to any strong truth of God firmly*
> *rooted in the mind, or contrary to any special*
> *bias of the mind. If the mind has a 'practical'*
> *bent, not visible foolish leading will be given;*
> *if the scriptures are well known, nothing*
> *contrary to scripture will be said; if the*
> *believer feels strongly on any one point, the*
> *'leadings' will be harmonized to suit that*
> *point; and wherever possible, will be so*
> *adapted to previously true guidance from*
> *God, as to appear to be the continuance of*
> *that same guidance . . . Satanic guidance*
> *alters the points of the life, and misdirects the*

energies of the man, and lessens his service value."[9]

DEMONS AND
THE CHRISTIAN

How far can evil spirits go in their work with Christians? Theodore Epp says, "Neither Satan nor any of his demons can possess anything that is possessed by Jesus Christ and the Holy Spirit."[10] This precept is an axiom that ought not to be forgotten. It will forever be true. Philip Davis, a missionary with extensive experience in demon activity, expresses the opinion that a Christian can become possessed with evil spirits. [11] However, the Christian's spirit remains untouched by the demons because the spirit has been given to God through salvation.

The Christian's body and soul ought to be also filled with the Holy Spirit. If the Christian is not Spirit-filled, he leaves himself open to the possibility of demonic possession. The believer is admonished in the Bible to surrender his entire being to God (Romans 12:1). If the believer insists upon being his own lord, he does so at his own risk. In I Corinthians 5:5, Paul instructed the Corinthian Church to "deliver such a one unto Satan for the destruction of the flesh, that the spirit may be saved in the day of the Lord Jesus." This verse ought to serve as a startling warning to any self-willed Christian.

SPIRITUAL DELIVERANCE

The Christian is not left defenseless. God is interested in the salvation of the mind and body as well as the spirit. He wants the "whole" man free. Therefore, God provides a means of deliverance. The answer lies in the filling of the Holy Spirit. This filling is accomplished through total identification with Christ. The "cross" is the answer.

A believer must identify himself with Christ and then he must maintain that identification. When Paul admonished the church to walk after the will of God, he was writing about identification (Colossians 1:9-10). Paul also wrote to the Church at Corinth instructing them to bring every thought into obedience to Christ (II Corinthians 10:4-5). Obedience is identification. Identification is a simple matter of trusting and obeying.

However, we want to know more precisely how to secure release from the bondage of demons. Many people today are vexed by demonic powers. Remember, we must be considered possessed if any area of our life is not under the control of the Holy Spirit. Regardless of the degree of bondage, we need deliverance.

DELIVERANCE FROM BONDAGE

Having discovered the activity of demonic power at work we must then follow Scriptural teaching for deliverance. We will consider both the one who is seeking deliverance and the one seeking to minister deliverance. Those seeking to help the afflicted must meet at least three conditions:

1. He must recognize the power of Jesus. Christ is the only one who has power and authority over demonic spirits. If this fact is ignored, failure will become reality.

2. He must have the unction of the Holy Spirit. The Lord Jesus Christ attributed His power to the Spirit of God. We too must have the sanction of His power in dealing with the underworld.

3. He must be cleansed from all known sin. Failure to confess sin and claim the cleansing power of Christ's blood will make one subject to demonic influence. One is living dangerously when he seeks to confront evil while known sin is in his heart.

This ministry of deliverance is most important and the one ministering must provide time for private counseling sessions. These private sessions present an opportunity for spiritual discernment. However, you must beware of becoming spiritually proud. Pride negates spiritual power! Christians must have godly compassion to help those who are possessed. Your goal is to lead the tortured soul to confess and forsake sin. Upon confession we must then lead them to denounce Satan.

Those who are suffering from evil spirits need God's deliverance. James 4:7-10 is the key:

4:7 Submit yourselves therefore to God. Resist the devil, and he will flee from you.

4:8 Draw nigh to God, and he will draw nigh to you.Cleanse [your] hands, [ye] sinners; and purify [your]hearts, [ye] double minded.

4:9 Be afflicted, and mourn, and weep: let your laughter be turned to mourning, and [your] joy to heaviness.

4:10 Humble yourselves in the sight of the Lord, and he shall lift you up.

These verses record a detailed procedure for resisting Satan and his demonic power. The key is "resistance." However, you must meet the requirements before you can resist. Resistance actually begins when the Christian turns to God in prayer (James 4:8a). Prayer is recognition of the problem. Prayer also recognizes that God is sovereign in all of the affairs of life and death. We must confess our sin to God (James 4:8b). This confession is a cleansing and purifying process that is accomplished through Christ's blood (I John 1:9).

Repentance is also involved (James 4:9). A godly sorrow for sin will be shown by the one who is genuine in his appeal. Then comes submission (James 4:10). Submission is the act of willfully submitting to another. To make the principle of submission personal, we must yield to His revealed will.

Having met these requirements, the believer now has the enabling power of the Holy Spirit to resist Satan. If by faith the believer claims the promise of James 4:7, Satan will flee.

The unbeliever (on the other hand) needs the help of Christians through whom God is working. It is obvious that they cannot deliver themselves. Medical science may offer some relief but science can offer nothing permanent against supernatural forces. Only Christ can offer a lasting remedy.

The common approach is to have the person ministering deliverance pray for the afflicted person's freedom. Then, in the boldness of God's power, command the demons to depart. Some demons are said to be more powerful than others. Therefore, under certain conditions prayer and fasting is often employed and maintained until deliverance has been accomplished. No doubt many have claimed success with the above process. However, as I study the New Testament for instruction on how I should engage in spiritual warfare in our post apostolic age, a different pattern emerges than the one stated above.

We must agree together about a couple of presuppositions before we can proceed. First, we must agree that the Gospels and the book of Acts are intended to communicate history. These books are historical in nature and should not be used to formulate doctrine. The book of Revelation is to communicate God's prophecy about the end times.

(These books just mentioned are written for the primary purpose of communicating the life of the Son of God and the transitional history of believers being brought out of Judaism to form Christ's Church. While these books may contain teaching points and some examples for holy living, these were never intended to be doctrinal instruction for Christians on how to live for Christ. Let me illustrate by referring you to John 3, where Jesus is interviewing Nicodemus. The passage clearly states that salvation is a mystery that may only be entered into through the "new birth." But it doesn't explore an explanation of the doctrine of salvation. We don't have a full exposition of that marvelous teaching until we reach the epistle of Romans. In Romans God gives us a detailed explanation of how He applies grace to man.)

The second thing we need to understand is that the epistles from Romans through Jude are designed by the Holy Spirit to teach believers how to walk after the Lord and how to conduct themselves in the church and in the world.

The above paragraph contains a premise that is essential to the following understanding of spiritual warfare and deliverance. Our premise is that Church doctrine must only be taken from the teaching epistles. For example, we are not told in any of the didactic epistles or books that believers are to take authority over demons and cast them out. We are told to submit to Christ, to resist the devil, to let the mind of Christ dwell in us, and to be transformed by the renewing of our mind.

As I have studied the evidence, it appears that those who are maintaining that Christians are to take authority over the enemy in the power of the blood of Jesus are doing so upon the assumption that we are recipients of apostolic authority. It is assumed that we have the same authority as those who held the position of "apostle" under Christ's leadership.

May I remind the reader that no one living today qualifies as an apostle in the same sense of those who bore that title after the resurrection of the Lord Jesus. There were two essential qualifications. One qualification was that the one serving as an apostle had to have been personally instructed by the living Christ. Another qualification was that an apostle had to be a contemporary of Christ. However, in that the word "apostle" means messenger, all Christians are apostles. But Christians today do not hold the "office" of "apostle" as those whom the Lord left to formulate and establish His Church. All evidence indicates that He endowed them with special powers to bear witness to their special message of salvation by grace through faith. These special powers gave evidence that their message was directly from God. History indicates that as the canon of scripture was being completed the powers of signs and wonders waned and finally ceased as an authenticating accompaniment to His message. Miracles have never ceased, for God can and does enter human history at His pleasure and void for the moment the laws of nature and we behold His miracles.

He may show His powers at any time (and He does). We now have a more sure Word of prophecy (The Word of God) to authenticate His message that Jesus Christ died to save all who--when believing--call upon His name. Therefore, He has not left us without instruction on how we (the Church) are to defend ourselves.

SPIRITUAL DEFENSE

The Church has been given the specific and appropriate armor to defend herself against Satanic attack. The Church must act both individually and corporately. Paul was given precise instruction for our protection and how it should be implemented. A description and the instructions on how to use the armor is found in Ephesians

6:11-18. Read carefully the passage below:

6:11 Put on the whole armor of God, that ye may be able to stand against the wiles of the devil.

6:12 For we wrestle not against flesh and blood, but against principalities, against powers, against the rulers of the darkness of this world, against spiritual wickedness in high [places].

6:13 Wherefore take unto you the whole armor of God, that ye may be able to withstand in the evil day, and having done all, to stand.

6:14 Stand therefore, having your loins girt about with truth, and having on the breastplate of righteousness;

6:15 And your feet shod with the preparation of the gospel of peace;

6:16 Above all, taking the shield of faith, wherewith ye shall be able to quench all the fiery darts of the wicked.

6:17 And take the helmet of salvation, and the sword of the Spirit, which is the word of God: 6:18 Praying always with all prayer and supplication in the Spirit, and watching thereunto with all perseverance and supplication for all saints;

The above text clearly shows us how Christ is our total defense in the affairs of life. He is our defense when doing battle with the princes of darkness. He is also our captain and defender when dealing with any set of circumstances which may have been created to tempt us. I use to think that the only valid application for the above text was that I (as a Christian) was responsible for consciously putting on each of the above pieces of armor. It was only then that I could have assurance of Christ's protection.

I later came to see that, in putting on Christ and walking after His Spirit, He actually becomes my protection and becomes my defense as each of the pieces of armor indicates. For example, He "is" my breastplate of righteousness; He "is" my shield of faith; He "is" my apron of truth, etc.

SUMMARY

The Christian must remember that Satan is a defeated enemy. He is subject to the Lord God. Therefore, the believer is not to face the devil with fear, but rather with boldness in the faith. [12] Each of the specific designations of the armor is to be taken as a protective measure against the adversary. This armor becomes effectual through prayer (Ephesians 6:18).

We conclude that God has provided a means for the Christian's defense against all demonic forces. Thus, the warfare rages until God, in His sovereignty, chooses to bring it to a close. In that hour of closure all sin will be dealt with and the glory of the Lord will be reestablished in the universe. Every knee will bow to Jesus and every tongue will confess Him as Lord.

Study Questions

1. How can evil spirits influence christians?

2. How may Satan influence the mind of man?

3. How may Satan influence the body of man?

4. Name some ways Satan uses deception as a ploy?

5. How does Christ become our armor against Satan?

NOTES
CHAPTER 8

1 Opinion expressed by Bill Gothard in a lecture at Keswick, N. J., January, 1969

2 Oswald Chambers, Biblical Psychology (London: Marshall, Morgan & Scott, Ltd., 1962) p. 47

3 C. S. Lovett, Dealing with the Devil (Baldwin Park, Calif.: Personal Christianity, 1967), p. 49

4 Opinion expressed by Joseph Carroll in amessage at Greenville S.C.

5 L. Gilbert Little, Nervous Christians (Chicago: Moody Press, 1956), p. 68

6 Theodore H. Epp, How to Resist Satan (Lincoln, Neb.: Good News Broadcasting Associations, Inc., 1965) p. 51

7 Raphael Gasson, The Challenging Counterfeit (Plainfield, N.J.: Logos International, 1966) p. 55

8 Jospeh Carroll, op. cit., opinion expressed.

9 Jessie Penn-Lewis, War on the Saints (Fort Washington, Pa.: Christian Literature Crusade) p. 81

10 Epp, op. cit., p. 53.

11 Opinion expressed by Philip Davis in a lecture at Greenville, S.C. , N.D.

12 Epp, op. cit., p. 72

Chapter IX

CURRENT EVENTS
AND EVIL SPIRITS

In a study of demonic activity you may wonder how evil spirits are currently showing themselves in our world. Do they reveal themselves as in the New Testament, or are they using new strategies to deceive our current generation?

My observation is that demonic activity has gradually increased over the past hundred years. The pressure of this activity has built to the extent that I expect an even greater satanic explosion. The ungodly activity of demonic powers has shown itself in religious cults, acts of apostasy, lawless world governments, social permissiveness, open ridicule of Christians and the Word of God, rebellion against authority, and an unusually potent revival of the occult and supernatural arts. The fact of diabolic activity can be shown through incidents which are currently forming human history.

Paul's Warning

Paul warned the young preacher Timothy to expect the work of evil spirits. He said that some who professed to believe would turn from the gospel in response to the message of deceiving spirits (1Timothy 4:1). These spirits are demons who teach the doctrines of their master the devil.

The early church faced a number of groups who had been influenced by seducing spirits. One example may be cited as the "Gnostics" who were followers of false teachings. What demons teach is not always bizarre. What they teach often appears godly.

The untaught or spiritually insensitive are particularly subject to their deception. However, truth with any mixture of error is error just the same. Many existing cults blend truth with error and the spiritual result is devastating. Paul even told the Corinthian Church that idol worship was in reality the worship of demons (1Corinthians 10:20). There is only one God! All other gods are mere creations of Satan and his demon hoards.

Examples Abound

An exhibition of demon worship existed in 1970 near Myrtle Beach, South Carolina. A few miles north of the city, between the heavily traveled coastal highway and the ocean was a spiritual retreat called "Meher Spiritual Center." It was founded at the direction of Meher Baba. Baba was a native of India who lived quite a normal life until he met one of the five "Perfect Masters of the Age." He was given "God - Realization." He later met the other four "Perfect Masters" and attained "Spiritual Perfection." He then began to gather disciples whom he trained in moral love and principles of compassion. He later claimed he was a direct manifestation of the living God. During the last forty-four years of his life, he maintained silence, claiming that enough truth had been given and that the world only needed examples of peace, love, and compassion.[1]

The caption headlining an article about the center was titled, "Spirituality Amid Worldly Myrtle Beach." The title is quite revealing, because, "The Center" illustrates (to the discerning soul) how Satan and his emissaries are working in our present world. Demonic activity is behind all worldliness as well as false religion and spirituality.

Scientology

One of the fastest growing religious sects in the world today is "Scientology." It is a religious mix of philosophy, humanism, and mysticism. Scientology draws its precepts from other religions and scientific disciplines and melts them together in a humanly pleasing order. In less than four decades it has grown to more than two million followers. In 1970 Scientology reportedly maintained twenty-five centers around the world.[2] This false blend of religion and science is another illustration of how evil spirits are using their doctrine to dupe millions of souls. Such activity reminds us of Paul's admonition not to follow every wind of doctrine (Ephesians 4:14).

Atheism

The avowed atheist, the late Madalyn Murray O'Hair,was reported to be a bishop. She established her own church and has named it "Poor Richard's Universal Life Church." The so-called church was chartered through a California mail-order scheme. Mrs. O'Hair's husband was appointed a prophet in the church. She named the alleged atheist, Mark Twain, The Patron Saint of Human Laughter.[3] This so-called church seems to be a tongue-in-cheek move on the part of demonic forces to ridicule the true church of Jesus Christ.

Evil spirits are not only at work introducing new religions, which are damning to the souls of mankind, but they are making inroads into the professing church. The true church (made up of all true followers of Jesus Christ) is being assailed on every hand. Satan and his evil hordes are energizing these manifold attacks. Every segment of society is ferociously assailing God's Word and the doctrines of the Faith. It appears to be open season on biblical Christianity.

Clergy Survey Reveals Satanic Influence

All Christians are open game as we make the transition into the new millennium. The Bible itself is being ridiculed as demon powers encourage man to reject the high moral standards of our holy God. The truth of the above observation is illustrated by the results of a survey taken by Western Reserve's sociologist, Jeffery Hadden.

Dr. Hadden contacted ten thousand protestant clergyman in the United States, asking them what they believed about various religious issues. Approximately seventy five percent of the surveys were returned. The responses to two or three questions will serve to make our point that evil spirits are influencing church leaders by attacking the authority of the Bible as divine revelation.

The first question we reference deals with what the ministers who responded to the poll believe about the personification of evil.

Do you believe in the devil and evil angels?
(The following of the various clergy respondents answered:"No!")
- 62% of Methodist respondents
- 37% of the Episcopal priests
- 47% of the Presbyterian clergy
- 33% of the American Baptist Convention clergy
- 14% of the American Lutheran pastors
- 9% of the Missouri Synod Lutherans

Do you believe in the verbal inspiration of the scriptures?(The following clergy respondents said: "No!")
- 82% of the Methodists ministers
- 89% of the Episcopal priests
- 81% of the Presbyterian ministers
- 59% of the American Lutheran clergy

We wonder how any minister of the Gospel, who believes in the authority of God's revealed Word, could ever have answered either of the above questions negatively. Therefore, we see the work of demons as they work among ministers who may often mean well, but are in reality nothing more than error struck prophets of satanic doctrine (2 Peter 2:1).

Those clergy who propagate liberal and modern philosophies at the expense of the clear declaration of God's Word are laboring under a false sense of scholarship. True scholarship is to be measured against the author of all truth who is Almighty God! The false prophets of the new scholastic order are deceived by the wicked one; regardless of their good intentions and grand delusions of enlightenment, they are still apostate teachers. They are the bane of the evangelical church and their teaching must not be tolerated. They must be loved for their soul's sake. However, we must reject their teaching for what it is: Satan's lies!

Evil Spirits and the Occult

Evil spirits are at work today in the area of the occult. Occultism in its various forms has become so popular that in some California high schools formal courses in occultism have been offered. One such course was taught in an English department and was called "Supernatural Literature." The teacher was Robert Beck, who invited people practicing occult arts to lecture the class. Beck had the students meet course standards by learning the vocabulary of the supernatural.[5]

All of the above was done under the guise of enlightened learning. However, when the ideas and principles of righteousness are presented as from the Bible, Christians are called narrow minded bigots. The reason biblical ideas are not allowed is because Satan has blinded the minds of those in charge and has caused them to believe that those postulating biblical truths are the enemies of mankind.

The Media

Magazines are continuing to flood the news stands with articles dealing with occult arts.[6] The supernatural element of evil is becoming more prevalent in television programming, where Satan and demons are often laughed at, indicating that he does not really exist. Then others exaggerate his ability and power so that no force in heaven or earth is seen as powerful as he. Of course, neither thesis is true!

Television and movie comedy routines deride those who take seriously God's admonition to "resist the devil and he will flee from you" (James 4:7,8). Public entertainment is progressively becoming more licentious,

163

which indicates that Satan and his emissaries are more than just active in our current world. Satan's rebellious nature is being transferred into our demonically influenced society where he is affecting human relationships.

He pits parent against children, children against parent, citizens against government, government against citizens, and nation against nation. No level of human relationship is exempt from his iniquitous influence.

Society and Evil

It seems to us that there has never been such an overflowing of wickedness as is witnessed in this present generation. Drugs, alcohol, and promiscuous attitudes toward sex, overtly used are all symptoms of a society which is greatly influenced by demonic forces. Demons have become bold and unrestrained in their dealings with humans. This unrestrained influence is seen in events like the massacre of Sharon Tate and her friends. The convicted murderers were members of a cult led by the now infamous Charles Manson. Manson had a strange hold on his followers and he called his harem a "family."[7] He closely patterned his perverted family after a group he read about in Robert A. Heinlein's Stranger in a Strange Land. The science-fiction novel by Heinlein was popular among the hippies of that period. It influenced Manson so much that he named one of his illegitimate children after the book's main character. He even chose to call his parole officer after the name of another of the book's characters.[8]

Lloyd Shearer, a feature writer, describes Manson as a counterfeit, traveling minister who quickly gathered a harem of naive young women into a converted school bus. Shearer says:

> *There, Manson sang, lectured, played the guitar, and made love to them in long-lasting, pleasurable sex sessions, "giving off lot's of magic." It was there too that these girls became subservient and obedient to his every whim, agreeing that he was "God, Jesus, Satan" or whatever he chose to call himself at the time.* [9]

Jean Stafford, another gifted writer, reports that Manson was interested in the occult and Scientology. Ms. Stafford also says, "The girls at present under arrest andmany others who had been members of his cult, said that Manson cast a spell over them, mesmerized them with his fervid eyes."[10]

Satan and the New Age

The rise of the "New Age" phenomenon has literally changed the religious face of our nation. At the turn of the century America was widely known for her evangelical religious understanding and commitment. Christianity's influence pervaded every segment of the social order. We must admit, that even by 1900, the church had become a mere shell of what Christ had taught she should be. Modern Christianity has bankrupted herself with her desire to be at peace with the prevailing winds of worldly wisdom. The "winds" have become more conflicting and anti-Christian with each passing generation. While seeking to be all things to all people, she has lost the respect of the very people she has sought to influence.

When Paul exhorted the church to use the all-things-to-all-people approach, his design was not to compromise Christian principles but to influence his world while maintaining a biblical separation. By comparison, our desire to be at one with the world has caused us to lose the world's respect. We lost respect by not striving to keep the standards taught by our Lord. We have become like the chameleon changing ourselves into whatever the social or religious landscape demands without regard for the teachings of Christ. We have done so in the name of peace and tolerance and we have accomplished neither.

What has caused the present impotence of Western Christianity? Why have we lost the spiritual power of the Whitfields, the Wesleys, the Puritans and Jonathan Edwards? Many would offer us a simplistic solution suggesting that Christianity has simply become irrelevant by being out of step with her culture. Some have seen the church as nothing more than a social agency designed and limited in a ministry to help the poor in their pain and suffering. Numerous ideas may be thrust forth about the real purpose of the church. These proposed solutions may have a measure of truth in them, but none of them really touch the central cause for loss of power with God and with man.

A more accurate view regarding the church's present spiritual condition, is that she has lost a sense of the moment-by-moment presence and power of the Lord Jesus. The early church had been infected by a dose of the undeniable presence of God's living reality. The loss of this dynamic presence did not come in one fell swoop. Her power receded in direct proportion to her willingness to compromise with sin. I see Moses' visits with God as a good example of what the church had experienced in those early days. You will remember that when Moses came down from his interviews with God, his face shone with God's glory. The longer he was out of the Lord's presence, the less his face glistened with the radiance of His glory. Likewise, when the church ceased to practice the presence of God, she began to lose the radiance of His grace and glory

Our spiritual enemy has masterminded the current state of affairs. Satan's ploy of intense persecution of the church in the first century has changed to the introduction of heresy through false teaching. He later introduced and caused the infusion of the tares among the wheat. These false professors of faith have caused an air of carnality to engulf many true believers. The process has continued through the centuries. The church has shamed herself by loving peace more than God's command to defend the Faith.

As the people of God, we have become a virtual nonentity because of our compromise of the Lord's truth. The void caused by our impotence has left people looking elsewhere for direction and meaning to life. The quest for meaning has led many people to turn to pop psychology and the occult such as astrology and horoscopes. Men and women across our nation have become mesmerized with having their fortunes read and foretold in the stars. Some believe the New Age movement and its emphasis on self awareness has been able to gain such a following because the Church has abandoned her mission of faithfully preaching the Gospel. Our nation entered the twentieth century flirting with humanism and agnosticism. Humanism as it is here used is the overt exaltation of man's interest in himself at the expense or neglect of God as creator. If God exists, agnosticism maintains that He is unknowable. Armed with these two foundational philosophies, Satan has used a number of strategies to deceive the people into abandoning the Jewish-Christian tradition upon which our nation was founded.

New Age is nothing more than a repackaging of pantheism and Eastern mysticism. The New Age philosophy has many facets and it is often difficult to get a handle on what they teach. But, "New Age" people have one central dogma: God is declared to be nothing more than the sum all things. He is not seen as the personal, holy, loving and compassionate Lord of the universe, but rather is said to be an impersonal force that inhabits all material compositions.

Satan is using one particular ploy to great effect in America. The strategy is to focus on the separation of church and state. On the surface it appears to be a fair and equitable policy. However, we may fail to take note of an important issue. Demonic forces have successfully led in the redefinition of the issue. The writers of the constitution clearly had in mind the restraint of government in the intervention of religion. Further, it is also obvious that the founders denied the sponsorship of a state religion. Demonic influence is using the humanistic and agnostic philosophy to redirect the emphases of the phrase "separation of church and state."

Humanistic thought has led to the obnoxious blatant attitude of self-centeredness. As a result our self-serving society has embraced materialism as her god. Materialism is nothing more than a love for the "things of the world." Only God can bring wholeness to man and it is the absence of His presence from our society that has brought about all our pain and servitude to Satan's ploys.

The feeling that man needs only education and dogged determination to acquire all his needs has led to humanism's bankruptcy as a philosophical world view.

Study Questions

1. What is the essence of Paul's warning about evil?

2. How does the clergy survey show the the influence of evil spirits?

3. How has Satan influenced the "New Age" movement?

NOTES
CHAPTER IX

1 Fred Trask, "Spirituality Amid Wordly Myrtle Beach," Sandlapper III (February, 1970) p. 11

2 Joseph Hopkins, "Scientology" Religion or Racket?" Christianity Today, XIV (November 7, 1969) 6.

3 Personalia, Christianity Today, XIV (February 27, 1970), 41.

4 News Sugary, "Divided They Merge," Christianity Today, XII (October 13, 1967), 48.

5 Associated Press Dispatch, "Spooks, Kooks- It's Part of Education," The Charlotte Observer, February 28, 1970, p. 16B.

6 For a more extensive treatment of the occult, refer to Chapter VI of this book.

7 Lloyd Shearer, "The Manson Family Murders," Parade, January 11, 1970, p. 6.

8 Behavior, "A Martian Model," Time, January 19, 1970, p. 44

9 Shearer, op. cit., p. 9.

10 Jean Stafford, "Love Among the Rattlesnakes," McCalls, XCII (March, 1970,69.

11 Eutychus, "Dear Observer of the Diabolique," Christianity Today, XII (February 16, 1968), 19.

12 Bob Larson, Rock and Roll: The Devil's Diversion (McCook, Neb.: Bob Larson, 1968) p. 95.

13 Ibid., pp. 84-86.

14 Statement by William Supplee, personal interview, March 1, 1970.

15 Merrill F. Unger, Biblical Demonology (Wheaton: Scripture Press, 1967) p.198

Chapter X

A SURVEY OF
EVIL SPIRITS IN
PROPHECY

The Bible clearly relates the doom of evil. Many of the details are not supplied, but the necessary information is presented. Evil spirits will play a major role as the period known the "great tribulation" approaches. The consideration of prophecy is important because it assures the believer of Christ's ultimate victory over the "enemy."

Approaching the subject of prophecy, we want to know what event will next appear on the prophetic scene. Scholars who hold to the "end times" position

175

called pretribulation premillennial believe the next historical event on God's prophetic calendar will be the rapture of the church (I Thessalonians 4:16-17). One of the most compelling reasons for believing the premillennial position is Paul's urgent appeal to watch for Christ's "imminent" return. Almost simultaneously with the rapture, we believe the "great tribulation" period will begin (II Thessalonians 2:3-8).

For our considerations, we will assume the premillennial view as the biblical view of the end times. (We know there are many godly and spiritual men who take a different view of the end time doctrines. If you are such a person, then please practice tolerance and allow this difference in theological interpretation.) Our study will not present a defense of premillennialism, but will simply use that system of interpretation to present the work of evil spirits in the last days.

The commencement of the tribulation will be a woeful series of events for those remaining after Christ has "caught up" His church. It will be woeful because, not knowing Christ as Savior, they will suffer God's judgments on Satan, sin, and unrighteousness. In one sense, the circumstances of that hour must be considered catastrophic.

THE TRIBULATION PERIOD

A discussion of Paul's second message to the saints at Thessalonica will give us a better understanding of the tribulation issue. Many of these believers were confused and upset. Why? Because, some had began to die and suffer persecution after Paul had given assurance that believing in Jesus would provide them eternal life at His coming. These saints had assumed some things that Paul

had never taught. It was assumed that becoming a Christian would protect against persecution and the ill will of the "world." They thought that since persecution was a present experience, the promise of the Lord's coming must be in error. But, Paul reminds them that there is a difference in the trouble or tribulation they were presently experiencing and the "trouble" of the "great tribulation." Consider Paul's instruction about this confusion in II Thessalonians 2:3-8:

2:3 Let no man deceive you by any means: for [that day shall not come], except there come a falling away first, and that man of sin be revealed, the son of perdition;

2:4 Who opposeth and exalteth himself above all that is called God, or that is worshipped; so that he as God sitteth in the temple of God, showing himself that he is God.

2:5 Remember ye not, that, when I was yet with you, I told you these things?

2:6 And now ye know what withholdeth that he might be revealed in his time.

2:7 For the mystery of iniquity doth already work: only he who now letteth [will let], until he be taken out of the way.

2:8 And then shall that Wicked be revealed, whom the Lord shall consume with the spirit of his mouth, and shall destroy with the brightness of his coming:

The only restraint now imposed upon evil forces is the hindrance of God's sovereign will and the ministry of the Holy Spirit's presence in the lives of His people. If it were not for His restraining hand, Satan and his demonic forces could surround the world with unchecked wickedness and debauchery. The "mystery of iniquity" mentioned in this passage is the ongoing work of satanic forces. It is a mystery because all the wiles and methods used by the devil have not been unveiled. However, when God removes the personality who is restraining Satan's activity, a great flood of wickedness will burst forth (II Thessalonians 2:7-8). G.Campbell Morgan refers to this person, who now hinders Satan, in the following remarks:

> *"The reference unquestionably is to the Holy Spirit, Who by His work of convincing the world of sin, of righteousness, of judgment, makes impossible the outworking of lawlessness to its ultimate degree. The time will come when the restraining influence will be removed, so that the mystery of lawlessness may be wrought out to its final*

178

expression, and that, in order that it may be destroyed by the unveiling of the Lord." [1]

During the period of tribulation, demon powers will be unleashed upon the earth.[2] Their work will be unhindered. For a season, it will seem that Satan and his emissaries will have accomplished their ultimate purpose.

On occasions, God uses evil spirits to judge the wicked of the earth. An eruption of evil spirits upon the earth to accomplish the judgement of God will take place as recorded in Revelation 9:1-11:

> *9:1 And the fifth angel sounded, and I saw a star fall from heaven unto the earth: and to him was given the key of the bottomless pit.*

> *9:2 And he opened the bottomless pit; and there arose a smoke out of the pit, as the smoke of a great furnace; and the sun and the air were darkened by reason of the smoke of the pit.*

> *9:3 And there came out of the smoke locusts upon the earth: and unto them was given power, as the scorpions of the earth have power.*

> *9:4 And it was commanded them that they should not hurt the grass of the earth, neither any green thing, neither any tree; but only*

179

those men which have not the seal of God in their foreheads.

9:5 And to them it was given that they should not kill them, but that they should be tormented five months: and their torment [was] as the torment of a scorpion, when he striketh a man. 9:6 And in those days shall men seek death, and shall not find it; and shall desire to die, and death shall flee from them.

9:7 And the shapes of the locusts [were] like unto horses prepared unto battle; and on their heads [were] as it were crowns like gold, and their faces [were] as the faces of men.

9:8 And they had hair as the hair of women, and their teeth were as [the teeth] of lions.

9:9 And they had breastplates, as it were breastplates of iron; and the sound of their wings [was] as the sound of chariots of many horses running to battle.

9:10 And they had tails like unto scorpions, and there were stings in their tails: and their power [was] to hurt men five months.

9:11 And they had a king over them, [which is] the angel of the bottomless pit, whose name in the Hebrew tongue [is] Abaddon, but

in the Greek tongue hath [his] name
Apollyon.

Demons, or evil spirits, will be enabled to take the form of locusts. This may be literal (actually becoming locusts) or it may be symbolically literal (becoming like locusts). Regardless of the case, whether of literal or symbolic interpretation, the plague is real and evil spirits are free to accomplish God's goals of judgment. It is important to note that the bottomless pit is literally the pit of the abyss which is the dwelling place of Satan and his demons.[3] The famous Bible teacher, Louis T. Talbot, maintains a symbolic interpretation is proper for this passage: "It is clear that we are to interpret the passage symbolically. But the spiritual plague does not strike down every man. Only those 'who have not the seal of God in their forehead' are to be stung by their damnable bludgeons." [4]

Mrs. George C. Needham reminds the prophetic student of one fact: "A symbol is always less than the idea symbolized." She also makes a pertinent comment concerning the Scripture above being considered:

"The locusts 'had a king over them, the angel
of the abyss: his name in Hebrew is Abaddon,
and in the Greek tongue he hath his name
Apollyon.' Their identity as demons is thus
established. They have power to materialize
after the hideous fashion described." [5]

181

Demonic forces upon the earth will vex mankind to the point that death will be desired, but they will not be able to die. The ones whom the evil spirits are not free to harm are probably Jews and Gentiles who have received Christ as their Messiah.

During this period of unusual tribulation, two distinctive, prophetic characters will appear on the world scene. The scripture clearly depicts these two men under satanic control. The first of these is referred to as "a beast" (Revelation 13:1). The "beast" mentioned here seems to be a man who has great political power (Revelation 13:1-10). The second personality is designated "another beast" (Revelation 13:11). He is portrayed as a religious leader who entices people to worship the first beast (Revelation 13:11-18).

Satan is clearly the mastermind motivating the work of these two world leaders. The evidence presented in the scriptures clearly shows that evil spirits aid the devil in his work. Therefore, we may reasonably conclude that during the tribulation demons are aiding these two satanic personalities in their work. The "great tribulation" will last approximately seven years. During this tribulation, intense persecution will be suffered by the Jews who have recognized and acknowledged the Lord Jesus Christ as their Messiah.

The world will face many plagues as a symbol of God's wrath. At the end of the tribulation period, Christ will return with an angelic host from heaven. Satan will marshal his forces against the Lord and His heavenly host (Revelation 19:19). A great battle will ensue; Satan and his army will be conquered. The devil will be chained and placed in the bottomless pit for a thousand years (Revelation 20:2-3). Evil spirits, being subject unto Satan, are also to be bound in the bottomless pit.

THE MILLENNIUM

After a period of one thousand years Satan and his demons will be loosed for a short time (Revelation 20:7). He will gather an army from the vast nations of the world and will press the saints of God. The account of Satan's last rebellion is recorded in Revelation 20:7-9:

20:7 And when the thousand years are expired, Satan shall be loosed out of his prison,

20:8 And shall go out to deceive the nations which are in the four quarters of the earth, Gog and Magog, to gather them together to battle: the number of whom [is] as the sand of the sea.

20:9 And they went up on the breadth of the earth, and compassed the camp of the saints about, and the beloved city: and fire came down from God out of heaven, and devoured them.

God will be victorious. Just as He has proclaimed His ultimate victory over Satan, it will become a reality.

Satan and his evil spirits will then meet their doom in the lake of fire.[6] They will be tormented in that awful anguish forever (Revelation 20:10). Then mankind will be forever free from the aggravation and the vexation of evil spirits. Every believer will have his ultimate purpose fulfilled because he will be like Christ. Every soul washed in the blood of the Lamb will spend eternity with God. Those without Christ will spend eternity in the "lake of fire" with Satan, whom they have served (Revelation 20:15).

Study Questions

1. Describe the "great tribulation."

2. How is that "great tribulation" different than tribulation in our present time?

3. What is the "millennium?"

4. When will Christ reign on earth?

NOTES
CHAPTER X

1 G. Campbell Morgan, Searchlights From the Word, (Westwood, N.J.: F. H. Revell company 1954), p. 355.

2 Opinion expressed by J. Dwight Pentecost, in a lecture (The Mystery of Lawlessness), Tape recorded lecture provided by Tapes for Christ, Dallas, TX, N.D.

3 R. Jamieson, A. R. Fausset, and D. Brown, Commentary on the Whole Bible, (London: Oliphants Ltd., 1961), p. 1552.

4 Louis T. Talbot, The Book of Revelation, (Grand Rapids: Eerdman Publishing Co., 1946), p. 127.

5 Mrs. George C. Needham, Angels and Demons, (Moody Press, N.D.), p. 113.

6 William W. Orr, The Mystery of Satan, (Wheaton: Scripture Press, 1966), p. 27. Evil Spirits in Prophecy

Chapter XI

EPILOGUE

We have sought to demonstrate through research the reality of evil spirits influencing the world and bringing evil upon mankind. The research was primarily biblical, but some of the material and information came from others who have either studied demonology or have experienced what they believed to be demonic powers through direct confrontation. Material directly relating to the subject was rather scarce. But, biblical accounts of demonic activity came alive through authenticated case histories, personal interviews, and testimonies of experienced missionaries.

Unless the person of Satan is considered, you cannot understand the purposes of evil spirits or the reason for evil. The Bible presents Satan as the personification of evil and the archenemy of our eternal God. The scriptures are not clear about the origin of demons. But, it is probable that demons were angels that rebelled against God and followed Satan. The rebel angels were expelled from heaven when Satan fell. The Devil was excommunicated from his exalted position as guardian over the throne of God. Evil spirits are so closely related in nature and character to Satan that it is difficult to imagine them apart from him.

Therefore, we may consider demons to be created beings like unto Satan whom they followed. When God condemned Satan, He, likewise, condemned the evil spirits. The origin and doom of evil spirits are the same as Satan's. However, we do not find a direct biblical statement regarding either the origin or doom of the demons who are currently free to roam the earth.

Evil spirits are indeed a biblical reality. Demonic reality is evidenced by the recognition given them by our Lord God. He acknowledged demons when He warned Israel not to traffic with them. Even the Lord Jesus Christ gave credibility to the existence of evil spirits when He encountered them during His earthly ministry. Every succeeding generation of the church has had a number of leaders who have acknowledged the reality of demons at work in our world. Evil spirits are discerned by Christians who believe the revelation of God's Holy Word.

However, for approximately two centuries the church has been hesitant about discussing the subject of demonic powers. This hesitancy is probably due in large measure to our emerging "age of reason." It almost seems that the church has been afraid to admit that demons exist. Social pressure in an enlightened era has probably added to her reluctance to acknowledge demonic reality. In my opinion, Satan has been the deceiving personality behind the church's silence and the world's denial. The devil does not want to be exposed, and he will utilize all his resources to avoid exposure.

In our current spiritual condition, Christ's Church, generally, knows nothing of the enemy she faces. However, it must be acknowledged that God has had His remnant of "truth" bearers in every generation that has maintained adherence to His Word. The average church member, when reading the Bible, does not realize the magnitude of the truth he reads. When reading a passage dealing with evil spirits, it simply does not occur to him that these spirits are real in the twentieth first century.

Every Christian ought to be aware of the magnitude and reality of demons. Unless we as believers are fully aware of our enemy, we cannot resist effectively while engaging in active spiritual warfare. It behooves each believer to become thoroughly familiar with the characteristics of demons. No war has been effectively fought by ignorant generals. Every highly regarded military force in the world trains its officers to learn all they can about their opponent. Even so the Christian soldier has a similar responsibility to discover all he can about Satan and his evil angels.

A demon's personality is essentially the same as Satan's. Therefore, the traits and characteristics of demons are essentially the same as Satan's. Evil spirits are personal beings who can think reason, feel, talk, and take action. They do not have bodies, but they are nonetheless real, discernible personalities. Demons, like Satan, are sinister, deceptive, malicious, fierce, and destructive. They are spiritual beings who are supernatural in their make-up, and they are members of a supernatural kingdom.

Evil spirits have supernatural power. They have power over the elements of nature, human beings, and certain circumstances. When allowed to exert their power, demons can influence the world and its inhabitants. Evil spirits have the power to inflict people with certain diseases and to take life under certain conditions. Restriction of their power is directly related to the sovereign purpose of God. I am of the opinion that demonic power has been revealed on a limited scale. God has not unveiled all the potential power of evil spirits lest we become overwhelmed.

Demons are active in a very real sense through occult arts. The believer is becoming more and more aware of the reality of evil spirits, as they manifest themselves through spiritism, magic, astrology, and various means of fortune-telling. Many of these areas have been thought harmless. However, through scriptural enlightenment and testimonies, it is evident to us that demonic forces are at work. It is spiritually dangerous for a Christian to involve himself in those things which God forbids. Evil spirits often use occult activities to gain control of a person's life. When one participates in the occult, even in the slightest degree, he leaves himself open to possible demonic possession.

Demon possession, as it is described in the New Testament, exists in the world today. Documented case histories and personal interviews have convinced us of demonic possession. Possession by evil spirits knows no geographical boundaries. The phenomenon of possession varies in degrees, depending upon the person and the circumstances surrounding the act of possession.

The writer concludes: A person is possessed of demons when an area of his life is beyond his own control. Hence, many people are under the power of demonic possession who are not aware of their condition. In this study, three degrees of possession were discerned: dormant possession, spasmodic possession, and total possession. The only lasting remedy from demonic control is victory through Jesus Christ. The Christian can, to some degree, be possessed by evil spirits. However, the believer is not at Satan's mercy, because God has provided an armor for his spiritual defense. We are convinced that Jesus is our defense.

Deliverance from demonic possession is effected through the power of Jesus Christ. Evil spirits are subject to Christ. When believers "walk in the light" they are clean through His blood and have His power upon their lives. The name of Christ is not to be used as a charm or magical formula. The name of Jesus Christ must be used in His behalf and for His glory.

God's people are engaged in a spiritual struggle with Satan and his army of fallen angels. Satan craftily deploys his forces in a manner most advantageous to his cause. It appears that demons aim their most potent weapon at the human mind. The devil's favorite and most powerful weapon in the satanic arsenal is deception. Evil spirits are so apt at their work that it requires a most discerning heart to know when they are active in one's life. Spiritual warfare is a difficult campaign because it is hard to recognize our unseen enemy. James makes it clear; resistance is the key to victory. The supernatural power of Christ becomes effectual in the Christian's life as he resists the devil.

The increasing intensity of evil on the world scene becomes apparent through the reported incline of the crime rate, racial hatred, strange interest in the supernatural, and widespread human antagonism evidenced in war. Evil spirits are largely responsible for giving energy to these activities, as they motivate the wicked hearts of men through the power of suggestion. Demons and evil will not prevail! God will, in His own time, signal for the victorious return of Christ. Christ will defeat all Satanic forces and cast them into the lake of fire which will ultimately be their place of judgment.

Our study is by no means exhaustive in its scope. However, we have attempted to present biblical evidence which will convince the "open" mind that evil spirits are real and are working in our world today. The only conclusive evidence, in the absolute sense, is found in the Bible. Other conclusions and opinions stated are purely the result of the normal process of reasonable deduction. We weighed the evidence in direct reference to a scriptural pronouncement and have found that the only reasonable conclusion is that believers are engaged in a mighty battle. We must fight this battle on a moment to moment basis until we are relieved of our duty by a call to report to heaven.

Even in heaven, the saints of God (believers) will continue to engage in the battle through what I call heaven based intercessory prayer. Jesus is engaged in that ministry now and I am convinced that it will become our ministry as well. We will continue until the battle is won and victory is proclaimed.

BIBLIOGRAPHY

Associated Press dispatch. Spooks, Kooks'- Its Part of Education" Charlotte Observer, February 28, 1970, p. 16B

Davis, Philip. Lectures at Greenville, S.C. Tapes available from W. D. Kennedy, Greenville, S.C.

Barclay, William. The Acts of the Apostles. Philadelphia: Westminister Press, 1955.

Behavior. A Martian Model, Time, January 19, 1970, p. 44.

Bounds, Edward M. Satan: His Personality, Power, and Overthrow. Grand Rapids: Baker Book House, 1966.

Buker, Ray B., Sr. Are Demons Real Today, Christian Life, XXIX (March 1968), 42-43.

Bunyan, John. The Holy War. London: Frederick Warne and company

Carroll, Joseph. Message at Greenville S.C. Tape available from W. D. Kennedy, Greenville S.C., ND

Chambers, Oswald. Biblical Psychology. London: Marshall, Morgan & Scott, Ltd.,

Coleman, Pauline. Personal interview. October, 1968.

Corwin, Margaret and Orland. Personal interview. August, 1968.

Davidson, F., A. M. Stibbs, and E. F. Kevan. The New Bible Commentary. Grand Rapids: Eerdman Publishing Co., 1955.

Demon Experiences in Many Lands. Chicago: Moody Press, 1960.

Edersheim, Alfred. Jesus the Messiah. New York: Longmans, Green, and Co., 1898.

Ellicott, Charles J. (ed.). Commentary on the Whole Bible. 8 Vols. Grand Rapids: Zondervan Publishing Co., 1959.

Epp, Theodore H. How to Resist Satan. Lincoln, Neb: Good News Broadcasting Associations, In., 1956.

Essbaum, Danwart. Personal interview. September, 1968.

Eutychus. Dear Observers of the Diabolique, Christianity Today, IXX (February 16, 1968) 19.

Gason, Raphael. The Challenging Counterfeit. Plainfield, N.J.: Logos International, 1966.

Larson, Bob. Rock and Roll: The Devil's Diversion, McCook, Neb.: Bob Larson, 1968.

Lewis, C S. The Screwtape Letters. New York: The McMillian co., 1966.

Little, L. Gilbert. Nervous Christians. Chicago: Moody Press, 1956.

Lockyer, Herbert W. All the Doctrines of the Bible. Grand Rapids: Zondervan Publishing House, 1964.

Lovett, C. S. Dealing with the Devil. Baldwin Park, Calif.: Personal Christianity, 1967.

Maclear, G. F. Old Testament History. Grand Rapids: Eerdman Publishing co., 1952.

Morgan, G. Campbell. The Gospel According to Mark. Westwood, N. J.: F. H. Revell Co., 1927.

_____. Searchlights from the Word. Westwood, N. J.: F. H. Revell Co., 1954.

Needham, Mrs. George C. Angels and Demons. Chicago: Moody Press.

Nevis, John L. Demon Possession. Grand Rapids: Kregel Publications, 1968.

News Summary. Divided They Merge, Christianity Today, XII (October 13, 1967), 48.

Orr, William W. The Mystery of Satan. Wheaton: Scripture Press, 1966.

Paxson, Ruth. Life on the Highest Plane. 3 Vols. Chicago: Moody Press, 1928.

Penn-Lewis, Jessie. War on the Saints. Fort Washington, Penn.: Christian Literature Crusade.

Pentecost, J. Dwight. The Mystery of Lawlessness, Tape available at Tapes for Christ, Dallas, Texas., ND

_____. Satan. Tape available at Tapes for Christ, Dallas, Texas., ND

_____. Trafficking with Demons. Tape available at Tapes for Christ, Dallas Texas., ND

Personalia. Christianity Today, XIV (February 27, 1970), 41.

Pipegrass, Charles. Demonism. Tape available at Tapes for Christ, Dallas, Texas.

Pierson, Arthur T. The Bible and Spiritual Life. Fincastle, Va.: Scripture Truth Book co. 1968.

Pike, Diane Kennedy. Bishop Pike's Triumph Over Death, Ladies Home Journal, LXXXVII (February, 1970), 71.

Pink, A. W. Gleanings in Exodus. Chicago: Moody Press.

Prince, Derek. Release from Depression,: Christian Life, XXIX (March, 1968), 67.

Scofield, C. Is. New Scofield Reference Bible, Ed. E. S. English. New York: Oxford Press, 1967.

Shearer, Lloyd. The Manson Family Murder, Parade, January 11, 1970, p. 6.

Stafford, Jean. Love Among the Rattlesnakes, McCall's, XCII (March, 1970)m 69. Story of Jane. N.D. Tape available from W. D. Kennedy, Greenville, S.C.

Strong, Augustus H. Systematic Theology. Philadelphia: Judson Press, 1945.

Supplee, William. Personal interview. March 1, 1970.

Talbot, Louis T. The Book of Revelation. Grand Rapids: Eerdman Publishing Co., 1946.

Thayer, Joseph H. Greek-English Lexicon of the New Testament. Grand Rapids: Zondervan Publishing House, 1962.

Thomas, David. Acts of the Apostles. Grand Rapids: Baker Book House, 1955.

Thomson, W. M. The Land and the Book. Grand Rapids: Baker Book House, 1966.

Toussaint, Stanley. Demonism. Tape available at Tapes for Christ, Dallas, Texas.

Trask, Fred. Spirituality Amid Worldly Myrtle Beach, Sandlapper, III (February 1970), 11.

Unger, Merrill. Biblical Demonology. Wheaton, Ill.: Scripture Press, 1967.

Van Baalen, Jan Karel. The Chaos of Cults. Grand Rapids: Eerdman Publishing Co., 1960.

Vine, W. E. Dictionary of New Testament Words. Westwood, N. J.: F. H. Revell Co., 1966.

Vos, Geerhardus. Biblical Theology. Grand Rapids: Eerdman Publishing Co., 1948.

Wilson, Dan. Personal interview. September, 1969.

Young, Robert. Analytical Concordance to the Bible. Grand Rapids: Eerdman Publishing company

Young, William B. Demon Activity. Goldenrod, Fla.: Worldwide Keswick.

Appendix I
Old Testament Examples
of Demonic Activity

The Worship of Demons

Leviticus 17:7

Deuteronomy 32:17

2 Chronicles 11:15

Psalm 106:37

Instances of Demon Possession

1 Samuel 16:14-23
It appears that Saul may have been possessed by an evil spirit.

Adversaries of Men

Judges 9:23
Demons caused the trouble between Abimelech and the Shecemites.

Demons & False Prophets

1 Kings 22:21-23
Demons gave the message to the false prophets.

Demons as Familiar Spirits

1 Samuel 28:3-7
We have a record of Saul dealing with a medium.

1 Chronicles 10:13-14
This passage records God's judgment upon Saul.

Demons & Magic

Exodus 7:11; 8:19
Demons energized the Egyptian magicians.

Daniel 2:4-7
The Chaldean magicians trafficked with spirits.

Demons & Witchcraft

Numbers 22:6; 23:23
Balaam conferred with those who engaged in supernatural arts.

2 Kings 9:22
Jezebel had priests who practiced witchcraft.

Naham 3:4-5
People in Ninevah were noted for dealing in sorcery.

Isaiah 47:9-13 Ezekiel 21:21-22
Babylonians were known for practicing evil art.

Appendix II
New Testament Examples
of Demonic Activity

Sacrifices Offered to Demons

    1 Corinthians 10:20

    Revelation 9:20

Witchcraft Forbidden

    Galations 5:20

    Revelation 21:8; 22:15

Witchcraft Practiced

    Acts 8:9 Simon of Samaria

    Acts 16:16 Maiden possessed by demon

    Acts 19:19 Event at Ephesus

Records of Demon Possession

    Matthew 8:28; 9:29; 12:22; 15:22; 17:15

    Mark 1:23; 5:2

    Luke 8:2

    Acts 5:16; 16:18; 19:12

Sorcery Practiced

    Matthew 24:24 False Prophets

    Acts 19:13 Vagabond Jews

    Acts 19:14-15 Sons of Sceva

Made in the USA
Columbia, SC
29 September 2017